In the Claws of
the Vulture

IN THE CLAWS OF THE VULTURE

A Remarkable Story

Marlene Patterson

Marlene Krepelka Patterson

Over the Transom Publishing Company
Fairhope, Alabama
2000

Over the Transom Publishing Company
323 De La Mare Avenue
Fairhope, AL 36532
email: info@overthetransombooks.com

In the Claws of the Vulture: A Remarkable Story
Copyright © 2000 by Maria Krepelka Patterson

All rights reserved under International and
Pan-American Copyright Convention.

Without limiting the rights under copyright reserved above, no part of this book may be reproduced or transmitted in any form or by any means, electronic or mechanical, including photocopying, recording, or by any information storage and retrieval system, without prior written permission of the publisher.

Library of Congress Catalog Card Number: 00-108904
ISBN 0-9643727-6-2

Manufactured in the United States of America

Typeset in Adobe OldStyle 7

Cover design by Marlene Patterson
Author's photo by Chris John, London Photography
Book design by Suzanne Barnhill, Words into Type

First Edition 2000

10 9 8 7 6 5 4 3 2 1

Acknowledgments

THERE ARE MANY PEOPLE who have touched my life and I remember them all in a very special way because they have contributed to the richness of my life's experience. This is to all of you who have held me up in quiet prayer to the Lord. To all of you who have financially supported me in fulfilling the call on my life. To all of you who have loved me enough to stand by me. There is not room to recount all my friends, my blessings. I thank you.

I want to give special attention here to my own wonderful family. This book is written for Carolyn, who, with her quiet resolve even in suffering, her good humor, and her big heart, loved us all. Carolyn, darling, some day we will again be united.

To Dale, who has been a good son to me and many times surprised me with his compassion for little and helpless ones, who had the biggest belly laugh even as a little boy, and who enjoyed the Lord's wide outdoors while growing up in Spanish Fort.

To Paul, who fought many battles within over the years and won by the grace of God. Your loving concern for me in the last few years has deeply touched me; to Kathy who has cared for me like my own daughter would.

This is written for you, Joey and Teenie, so that someday you will remember your Oma as a person who loved the Lord, her family, her friends, and life. Be strong, be honest, be open to Jesus. All of you have a part in this book, because by rubbing against the fiber of my life, you see before you this human being that the Lord God has seen fit to call His own.

I thank you all and love you for it.

Table of Contents

	Acknowledgments	v
	Preface	ix
1	The Beginning	1
2	The Storm Clouds Gather	5
3	Papa and Mama	9
4	Home	19
5	Family	27
6	Banners and a Spirit	33
7	The Ugly Black Vulture	37
8	The Claws Tighten	43
9	Sadness and Confusion	47
10	Caught in the Conflict	53
11	Leaving Familiar Places	59
12	The Nightmare	63
13	The Granite Building	73
14	Coming Home	81
15	The Search	89
16	The Convent School	101
17	Learning Flexibility	109
18	America	115
19	A Full Family	123
20	The Renewal	133
21	The Next Generation	137
22	The Call	143
23	Freedom	147
24	Coming Full Circle	153
25	Mission: Eastern Europe	157
26	A New Beginning	161
	Epilogue	171

Preface

I AM A CHILD OF THE TWENTIETH CENTURY and the Spirit of this Age was alive and had power when I was young—as it has now. I have seen it in families, in schools, in governments, in marriages. It comes in different forms. Perhaps not as blatantly as during the "hot summers" in the fifties or the rebellion of the sixties. It seems more "civilized" than during the years of Hitler and World War II.

Even though many years have passed since I was young, and much has happened in the world, on my last trip to Eastern Europe I saw things quite similar to what we dealt with during and after the Second World War. The human condition has not changed. It doesn't seem to matter where one is and what the date is—Kosovo, Boston, Bulgaria, Chicago, or anywhere else for that matter.

Going about my business while stationed there, in different parts of the world, I have received a glimpse of this spirit again and again: in Russia, in Bulgaria, in Albania, in Romania, in Austria, in East and West Germany, and in the United States. There is one truth that is inevitable: those who ignore history and get caught up in that spirit will sooner or later be destroyed. The snare that is set up before us is more powerful than the jaws of a hungry lion. It is a snare that destroys people from within; one that does not easily loosen its grip. Only through the power of the Living God can one be delivered.

Kosovo—April 1999
It is raining. All around me is unrest. Oh, just a few hundred yards more and I will be in Albania; perhaps someone can help me there! The pain! Come on, little one, wait just a little longer; there is no place to lie down here; there is no privacy. They are all just milling around me and staring; I wish they would help me! I am so thirsty! Is there no one here to give me shelter? Must my child be born in this awful no-man's-land? Where is my husband? Did they kill him? Will I ever see him again? Will someone be able to be with me? I am so afraid....Oh, God!

CHAPTER 1

The Beginning

VIENNA, AUSTRIA, MARCH 20, 1930—It was a clear, early spring morning when I first saw the light of day. Joy reigned for Barbara and Karl at the arrival of their second child, a healthy girl. My given name was Maria Magdalena. All my life my parents called me Marlena, a contraction of my full name, and now I go by Marlene.

In New York there was unrest because of the many unemployed. Communists and police battled in the streets as they had earlier this year in Germany and other European countries.

In Rome the Pope—Pius X—celebrated a special mass for the churches in Russia who were being oppressed.

Hitler's Party would prove to be stronger than the Communists in the German Parliament later that same year.

※

I grew up in an average and culturally middle-class family in Vienna. Even though we were not blessed financially as the middle class is today, we always had what we needed. By today's standards you might have called us poor. I did not know. Nobody told me I was poor. I was content.

I was a strong-looking little girl with strawberry blond hair, braided in pigtails, that reached below my waist. Perhaps I was a bit of a tomboy because every one of the pictures I have of myself at that age show that I had a bandage on either my knee or my arm. In fact, I recall, not a fence was too tall or a tree too high that I did not at least try to conquer it. Always curious about the world about me, I am sure I was a challenge to my parents. Popularity was not one of my desires because I seemed to be content pursuing the interests I had. I had three friends in my childhood as I remember: Traute, who did not return the fondness I felt for her,

Evi, who maintained the same kind of thinking patterns I had, and Lissy, who was simply my buddy. We had fun together and on occasion got into mischief.

Perhaps today I would be considered a semi-loner. I made all A's in school and was eager to learn and to please my teacher whom I dearly loved.

Frau Ullman was a very special teacher. She taught us to think and question everything we learned, so that we could get it straight in our own head, and be sure of what we believed and thought. After going to Volksschule (elementary school) for four years I took the test for the eight year Gymnasium (a combination of junior high and high school). I passed and was enrolled in a higher school of learning that prepared us for entrance into the University. It was a demanding school with little frills except for sports events of the Hitler Youth that we were obligated to partake in. I remember Mama saying that my job was to study and do well in school. So at the giant age of ten years I was introduced to English, Latin, biology, history, geography, physics, chemistry, and mathematics, not to mention German, music, and art. I was to carry these subjects for the next eight years. It was not an easy youth but I never felt unhappy. Often my studies became difficult because of the frequency of the bombing attacks during the war years.

I was the second of three children. My older brother Karl had died of pneumonia as a baby because antibiotics were not yet a miracle cure. When I was nine years old my younger brother Helmut was born. He and I really never had a chance to get to know each other because of all the unrest, the bombings, and later on the evacuations. To me he was my little brother, whom I took care of at times under Mama's watchful eyes. I guess I was typically selfish and Helmut was a typical younger brother, often a nuisance to me. He was a joy to my parents in their later years. It has only been in recent years that we have rediscovered each other, and it has been a blessing.

Traditions were important in my home, especially during the holidays. There was sort of a security in knowing exactly how it was going to be at Christmas or at birthdays. Not that there never were surprises, but we looked toward the predictable with an anticipation that was fun. What we ate on Christmas Eve, for instance, or how Papa would traditionally trim the tree. I remember my family's love for music. There was always music, the beautiful classical music of the great composers, and there were always books. But now I am getting ahead of myself.

CHAPTER 2

The Storm Clouds Gather

Have you ever been in a lightning storm? It begins with the lightning on the horizon, seemingly far away, and then all of a sudden it is here! There is almost a smell of danger in the air. The hair on the back of your neck stands straight up. The energy unfurled is awesome. That is how it was in the thirties in Austria.

Right across the border, in Germany, changes were taking place also. The Nazi Party had more than doubled their seats in the Reichstag the previous year. Hitler was named Chancellor of Germany; Goering and Frick were given cabinet seats. The scene had been set for an enormous upheaval right in the center of Europe.

On my third birthday, on the twentieth of March, Hitler opened the first concentration camp: Dachau. Three days later on March 23, 1933, Hitler was made Dictator of Germany. Almost immediately the horror started. Jewish stores were being boycotted. They began to burn books that were "dangerous to the Reich." On June 26 a law was passed to "purify the Aryan race," and by the end of August thousands of Jews were put into concentration camps. For the first time the name Heinrich Himmler came into prominence as he was given authority over the operation of concentration camps.

In Austria, Chancellor Dollfuss was murdered by the Nazis during July of that year. I was just a little girl, but I remember the sound of exploding grenades very near to us and later saw the big holes in the walls of some of the apartment houses in Vienna's fifth district: artillery. There had been a revolution.

On the nineteenth of August, 1934, just seventeen days after Germany's President Hindenburg's death, Hitler was "voted" in by 90 percent of the German votes as President and Chancellor of a highly motivated people. In short, he was made the most powerful person ever in the history of man.

But this was just the beginning. The ravenous vulture had begun to attack.

Three more concentration camps opened in Sachsenhausen, Buchenwald, and Lichtenburg (a women's camp). In the fall of 1937, the review of 600,000 men of the armed forces parading before Hitler in Nürnberg showed his power growing day by day.

In November of that year the Waldenbergs' children were taken from their parents because they refused to teach Nazi ideology to them. They were from a religious sect called the International Bible Researchers (Jehovah's Witnesses). The first victims of their religious convictions.

The dawn of 1938 brought a new shock to the European people. Hitler promoted himself to be the military chief over all the German troops. Nothing now stood in the way of the takeover of other European countries.

Austria would be the first. The referendum called by the Austrian chancellor was canceled by the Minister of the Interior, Arthur Seyss-Inquart, on the order of the German dictator. A triumphant Hitler viewed from his mountain top retreat at Berchtesgaden, high above the Border-City of Salzburg, the mass of German troops ready to strike. Confronted with this manifestation of power, and wishing to stop a possible blood bath, the Austrian Government gave in and signed over my country.

It did not matter that the last Hapsburg Emperor, Otto, campaigned against Hitler from his exile in France. His political sympathizers were quickly incarcerated.

Like a treacherous, low swirling fog fear entered my beautiful Austria.

On the fourteenth of March, 1938, I watched from my uncle's apartment at the old Hapsburg castle as Cardinal Innitzer of Vienna, the highest-ranking representative of the Catholic Church in Austria, embraced Hitler in a gesture of official friendship amidst the cheers of thousands. There were flaming torches that had become so popular. This day the ever-familiar "Grüss Gott"—God's greetings—would be replaced with the very official "Heil Hitler" for the next years.

We did not yet recognize that there is no way to compromise with a dictator. Lightning had struck, and the smell of sulfur was in the air. How quickly would the dry, stripped straw begin to burn? We did not know what was ahead. My world had been turned upside down.

Miami, Florida

This place is nothing like Havana, Cuba! I dreamed of coming here to be free. I am glad I came, and yet, I am saddened because I have not heard from home. The last time I saw my family I was boarding the small vessel to take me to the United States. I wonder if they are well. I pray Mama doesn't worry about me. And I hope Pa' is really teaching Juan how to get along. Juan is so young. He must have grown a lot since I left. Oh, Pa' make sure he knows how hard it is to get along by yourself in the midst of strangers. Teach him to work hard. I wish I could see all of you. I am so homesick for the people I love.

CHAPTER 3

Papa and Mama

LET ME INTRODUCE YOU TO MY LOVED ONES. My father, Karl, was a very gentle and loving man. He was a chemist. He was short and stocky and very athletic. He loved to play soccer and climb mountains. Often he took me with him into the mountains until my younger brother was old enough to go with him. We would hike up high into the Alps. There he would show me all the beautiful flowers and grasses and the majesty of the snow covered peaks around me. We would admire the Edelweiss, the blue Enzian and, the red Alpenrose. We commented on how nature made up for the short season of warmth by the intensity of the color in all the flowers.

I remember watching the night shadows in the valleys become brighter and brighter until the sun appeared in all its glory. An unforgettable sight at 4500 feet or more. I remember the beauty of it was so overwhelming that I thought my chest would burst—much like the feeling of succumbing to the worship of the Most High. I remember him pointing out how insignificant we really were.

Papa was always clean-shaven, with black hair slicked back because it was so straight. The silly way he wrapped a towel around the wet hair! It made his hair slicked down for the rest of the day when he took it off. It always reminded me of some foreign dignitary with his twisted turban.

He wore, according to the fashion of the day, the most ridiculous sock garters and stiff high collars on his shirts, that could be taken off, cleaned, stiffened, and worn again. Mama would take the collars to the cleaners and exchange them for clean ones.

He loved his children with a love that spoke few words. He really enjoyed surprising us with gifts he had made himself.

Once, he made a wooden doll kitchen for me and convinced me that he was working on a stove for the kitchen—he was! For my doll kitchen! At Christmastime we received one toy and the ever-traditional new mittens. Papa, in turn, must have had half a dozen handmade key rings. He always managed to display their usage to stimulate our pride.

Your Santa Claus, or St. Nikolaus, as we called him, was a fellow that came earlier at the Feast of All Saints and All Souls. He brought goodies and little presents to good little girls and boys. He gave the not-so-good ones a good talking-to. He wore a tall bishop's hat and a robe that was shining white with gold trim. In his hand he had, as it seemed to us, an over-dimensional long shepherd's staff.

With him came a fellow called Krampus. He looked like a devil with horns and a tail. All black and evil-looking. He carried with him a switch made of willow branches. The children that had not been good felt the sting of his switch. We children used to hate him because he showed up at the most unusual times and places. Like meeting us on the way home from school when it was already dark, wet, and cold outside. I never did like Halloween for that reason. It reminded me too much of the fear we had while walking home from school.

Christmas Eve was set aside for Christkind (Christ child). Papa seemed to somehow have a special permit with Christkind on Christmas Eve. Every year there was the all-familiar hush of anticipation as he disappeared into the dining room, closing the double door behind him. The sound of crinkling paper and the occasional sound of a tinkling bell almost took our breath away! He was absolutely the best when it came to trimming a Christmas Tree. There were always real candles and sparklers. Papa always gave the credit to the angels who did the work, and made sure there was a lock of angel hair for us to find on the floor near the tree. We never tired of it! Christmas Eve! That was the time the Christkind brought gifts to all of us.

My parents loved music and enjoyed singing around the house. From them we also learned to value books. In the evening after supper we would settle around the big eating table. While Mama and I did needlework and my brother played with his toys, Papa would go to the large bookshelf, pick out a book and settle down to read to us. Oh, he knew how to read the stories of Indians, trappers and maidens in distress in such a way that you felt you were there right in the middle of them. Places without roads—only rivers and fords to cross—where one hiked through the woods. Places with mountains higher than the Alps; of rivers with great big waterfalls; of cities so large, with buildings so tall, that one had to lean way back to see the tops of them. There were books of jungles filled with strange birds and mighty hunting animals; of deserts that went on and on, so a person got weary just looking! To each one of the characters Papa managed to bring life.

Often when closing our eyes we would imagine how it would be to be there. We heard of travels to China; stories that told of heroes, of nations, and faith. Stories of the world around us and of people and places far away to stir up our imagination. How wonderful it would be to travel to see all the delightfully exciting countries he read about! I guess it was sort of a home schooling in geography, history, and science. That is where I first heard in detail about a place called America.

My Papa had a special love for the sounds of different languages. He was a gifted linguist. When he was a young man and newly married to Mama he took a job in Milan, Italy. He worked at a large bank house where he filled the job of an English correspondent. They lived there till Mama became pregnant with my older brother. Then they returned to Vienna. My Papa is the one who made me curious about how it would be to communicate in another language with people from another country. If I have a talent for languages, it is an inheritance from Papa.

This smart and humble man had a quick laugh. He was never too tired to pay attention to us. I always felt he could do anything. He was sort of larger than life to me. Papa only needed to look at us cross and we scurried.

When Hitler's regime called him and others back into the service, I was proud of him. He never said how he felt. He was neither eager nor reluctant. It was something that had to be done, I suppose, so he did it. I didn't know that it grieved him to see the destruction everywhere, and I don't believe he ever forgot the horror of Warsaw. Until then, I think he wanted to give the benefit of the doubt. Something broke in him there. When he came home on furlough from Poland, he never wanted to talk about it, ever.

As I look back, Papa and Mama were not deceived; they knew, but there was precious little they could do about it. So I suppose they hoped and prayed that it would all go away, and soon. There was not only fear but also seeds of distrust everywhere. Parents were afraid to speak out any criticism regarding the leadership or the government. Children were being asked very clever questions, at school and other places, and they unwittingly betrayed their parents and the conversations within the family.

Things were never discussed at home, at least not in front of the children. Since I have traveled into some of the former oppressed countries as an adult, I have begun to understand that the power of this horrible oppressive spirit is so strong when experienced in its full strength that it somehow renders you helpless. It is evil personified. Only people with a name and money and power were able to be heard. Many of them were killed for it subsequently.

There it was again: the fear. A byproduct of a dictatorship. What at first seemed to be an exciting adventure became a frightening nightmare.

The unpopular job of child discipline was my mother's lot. It is due to her diligence with this unpopular task that I have learned to be disciplined and to walk steadily even in the midst of confusion. We all were Roman Catholic but did not always piously observe the rules and regulations of the Church. My mother's faith was alive, and I often remember her praying for me as I left the house, marking my forehead with the sign of the cross.

Mama was short, comfortably plump, with blue eyes and always tousled-looking short auburn hair. She loved to cook for her family and friends. She was a good imaginative cook, who could make potato soup without salt or butter taste delicious. She had to at times when there was not enough to eat. I remember her taking one chicken breast and somehow stretching it to make a meal for the whole family by inventing a new recipe.

When my Mama worked in the kitchen she moved about in short, energetic steps, quickly accomplishing the most wonderful-smelling concoctions. I used to marvel at how Mama added a pinch of this and that, cocking her head to the side as she tasted the goodies. She never used a cookbook unless she was making some very difficult recipe, or one of Opa's marvelous tortes.

In the winter months when there were no fresh fruits and vegetables, because of the growing seasons, we ate a lot of kale and cabbage. These vegetables had much vitamin C in it. We had to; we were totally shut off from other countries that might have fresh grown food during the cold months. Oranges and bananas were not known by most children. I never had orange juice until I was almost twenty years old.

The kitchen was definitely her domain. She ruled in it! It had no frills in it. A working place. Only once do I remember a non-utilitarian item in it. It was a silly-looking frame that framed a new calendar every year. The corner grocery store gave them to their customers for Christmas gifts. The radio she wanted in there for her amusement had to be moved to the living room. "Too big," she sadly agreed. In this, her domain, she wore bright-colored aprons in the summer and more subdued ones in the winter. But one always wore an apron in the kitchen!

If you had ever looked into Mama's purse you would have named it "Open Sesame"! She was never caught off guard. Out of the depths of her mini-suitcase she could produce goodies and toys on our visits to the park, or medicine if we were mending from some ailment. It seems there was a rule: if medicines were not horribly bitter and foul-tasting, they surely could not make you well.

How we hated the inevitable medicine time when we were ill. Papa's charm would trick us when he gave us the medicine. He would tell us it was "Liquirizi" and the mere sound of it made us shudder. If we protested, he produced another bottle with a liquid that looked suspiciously the same but actually was called "Aquarella"! What a difference that made! It even sounded cool and more palatable. But Mama would say, remember how well you will feel tomorrow, because you have taken this today. A lesson well learned.

I believe she lovingly enjoyed serving her family. A real gem. Even as she got older Mama still did all her own housework. We children were sent to run an errand many times to help out. However, she did the ironing, mending, cleaning, cooking, grocery shopping, everything with the exception of doing the family laundry.

There she had help of a "washerwoman". Frau Marta—that was her name—came once every three weeks and did all the ceremonial washing procedures. Today, when with a punch of a button, one has either hot or cold water, large- or small-capacity washing, damp or extra-dry laundry, it is inconceivable that this hardworking soul came at about 4:30 a.m. and started to light the fire under the huge boiler.

When the water in it boiled, the white laundry that had been soaking since the night before was boiled in it. Then, with a wooden instrument, the laundry was transferred to a big tub to cool off, so it could be scrubbed on the washboard. (You know, I am talking about those funny squiggle-looking boards that people today are using for decoration in a "country kitchen"). From there, it went into the first rinsing tub, then into the second tub, where some bluing had been added to give the laundry that extra "white" look. It literally shone. Then it had to be taken to the yard to dry in the summer. To the attic in the winter and on rainy days. From there on Mama would take care of it. We would help bring it in and she would then do the ironing.

Old Marta and I were good friends. I always brought her snacks and lunch. Then I stayed to chat. She worked for us for many years. On laundry days, Mama would serve soup. Bowls of the most delicious, steaming soup and after it great big wonderful yeast dumplings, filled with homemade jellies and spiced fruits, topped with brown butter and sugar.

I remember many household chores that no one bothers with any more! Let me tell you: you have not lived if you have not had the experience of the "Betten Lüftung"—the airing out of the bedding. Almost daily, the bedding was piled in an orderly fashion on the very broad windowsills, so the sun would shine on it. Our house always smelled like sunshine and fresh air, like apples and spices. Even today, when I make apple strudel, I can close my eyes and almost smell the smell of my parents' home.

Mama never complained about too much work or even talked about being tired. She did what had to be done for a family. I don't know if she ever *felt* unappreciated. If she did, I never heard about it. Mama, or "Mutti" as we used to call her when we wanted something out of the ordinary, was a relaxed person who was sharp and alert to what went on around her. Yet of all the things she knew, she never burdened her children, unless it was good for our education or necessary for our survival.

She maintained strict discipline in the home and with a shake of her finger she said things that didn't make much sense to me then but hold a lot of truth for me now. "God saw to it that the trees don't grow into the heavens." Oh, I guess I got too big for my own good! I never felt I had to "compete" with her and I never was a threat to her. Even in my teens I stayed in line because of the consequences and because it was expected of me.

She, on the other hand, like a protective lioness, would leave us as much room as we could handle, and yet in strength and toughness she would watch over us. She would not allow us to do things in private that would not stand the scrutiny of public view. She set a standard for us. Raising kids was mostly women's work. Mama never decided on a course of action and then changed her mind. She knew no maybe. Crying, tantrums—only tried a few times—begging, manipulating would just make her more determined to enforce discipline. When Mama shook her head, it was *no*. It was kind of good to know exactly where you stood with her, even though we did not like it.

She had Papa's support in all decisions concerning the children. He was the last authority in our home. I guess the worst thing we could have done was to make Papa ashamed of us. Papa I could wrap around my finger; for Mama I always toed the line. Papa might have made me a softy; Mama made me tough. Together they nurtured us and formed our character, instilling in us a sense of integrity and a security that is very hard to explain.

You see, I never remember very many spoken words of love, as we would now express to our children, yet I knew without the shadow of a doubt that I was very much loved. The love expressed by whatever means was very much unconditional. In the last few years, I have understood that it is not important that a child know how a parent instills this security in them, only that they do. As I grew older and looked for security in God, it was very easy for me to transfer the trust I had in my own earthly father to the Father in heaven. How we loved them both, Mama and Papa!

Kosovo, April 1999

I am so weary. It is so hard to sort out my thoughts. The house—warm, bright full of life—what happened to it? Is it still there, or have the bombs and the soldiers taken it as a triumphant victory over us? Why? What happened to all of us? Will I ever be back there? and will my children ever again live in a real home?

How I loved the quiet of our garden in the early morning, watching the sun rise. Who is reading our books? Are they still there or were they burned along with the building? I don't even know where part of the family is! Is everything gone?

CHAPTER 4

Home

VIENNA, 1939—How beautiful were the early quiet hours in my home. It overlooked a lovely garden filled with filtered light of the morning sun. How I loved to sit and dream.

Here I was. In my room at my big desk doing homework. Soon I would be going into the Gymnasium (high school). I wondered how it would be in the new school. Would I make new friends, I wondered. Dreamily I counted the flowers on the silky white-and-blue-striped wallpaper, and as I looked around I could see my comfortable large daybed with its shiny wooden arms and all the nice new cushions Mama had bought for me that year. No wonder I liked to snuggle into my large rocking chair, it looked so inviting. How often I just got a book from the large bookcase to read and dreamed of all the places in the world I would like to see. I never wanted to give up my books!

How wonderful it would be to see the mighty Mississippi or travel down the Nile River in a large pleasure ship! How high the Andes must be and the mountains in Tibet! I could not imagine anything even higher than the Alps.

One cold February day as I enjoyed myself in my chair, Papa came in all excited. He told me to stay put and wait for him. I surely had never seen him that excited before and I wondered what was up. He had whisked Mama away and I began to be concerned. The minutes ticked away and when it began to get dark I got up and drew the dark blue drapes over the lacy curtains.

My Jewish neighbor Frau Liebl, whose grandson was like a brother to me, popped in and brought me a bowl of tasty soup and some nice hot tea. It felt good to see the steam rise from the little tea table. How chilly it had gotten in here! And where were Papa and Mama?

All of a sudden, I remembered that they had talked about a baby, my new little brother or sister, that was expected soon. Could it be? I felt a sigh of relief rising within me. Tomorrow. Tomorrow will be another day. So I finally opened my old-fashioned armoire and changed for the night. "Tomorrow," I murmured, sinking into my featherbed and falling into a sound sleep.

Oh, how bright the sun rose that next crisp morning, sending patterns, dancing through the lace curtains, into my room. I squinted into the sunny morning. I lazily stretched and yawned on awakening. Papa, who had opened my curtains, was smiling even brighter than the sun, or so it seemed. "Marlene, you have a brand new baby brother. Would you like to see him? His name is Helmut." A baby!? What does one do with it?

That was a short time ago. In February 1939. The house began to smell from chamomile and baby powder; on rainy days a long clothesline spoke of the fact that a baby lived her; mountains of diapers had to be folded every day.

All this had happened just a month before my ninth birthday and now we all were looking forward toward Easter. It was time again to polish all the furniture and carefully wash all the treasures of the family that were proudly displayed in the Biedermeier vitrine. Each item was carefully removed and washed or dusted and then returned. This had been my job for several years, and each year I looked forward to it eagerly, almost like meeting old friends. There were cut-glass bowls and fragile cups and saucers made out of exquisite china. There were glasses that rang like bells when one flicked them with a finger. I was taking good care of these cherished, wonderful treasures. Oh, I was important, all right!

And in the living room the grand piano had to be dusted, and on the doors all the brass knobs had to be polished. Just one more week to Easter. We had to shake out the heavy covers that were hung in front of the double windows, reaching to the floor. They kept the cold air out in the winter and so did the funny-looking pillows that went between the outer and inner window. They had to be removed. Spring finally was approaching!

How I loved to take off my slippers and slide in my socks on the shiny wooden floor. Mama never did like that too much! I looked forward to the fun things my family would do in the spring; like hiking in the mountains and playing soccer and visiting the zoo. What fun! But now we had some more work to do. Mama really needed me now since Helmut had arrived.

Little did I know that there was a trap put into place over all of us in Europe, which would once and for all put an end to my carefree life. We would be like birds in traps of the bird-catcher. There was no mercy on the ones caught. Once the trap snapped shut there was no escape. That was the design of the merciless creature. It flapped its huge wings over us, ready to strike, but God...

෫

I had a big family. Let me tell you about them. There were Oma and Opa, my father's parents. They owned a sweet shop. After they retired, they leased it out to a younger baker. Fortunately for us, Mama had learned some of Opa's trade secrets.

Opa's Konditorei (sweet shop) was located on the Ringstrasse close to the old Hapsburg palace. The gentlemen and ladies from the court used to come to get a piece of the famous Sachertorte and a cup of Melange (coffee) for their afternoon Jause (tea time). The Sachertorte, named after the Hotel Sacher where it was first made, was a cake of dark chocolate. It was moist and topped with a semisweet glaze that just melted in your mouth. Mmm, I can almost taste it when I think of it. Doesn't it sound romantic? Vienna! Mama told us, how she used to help out in the sweet shop when she first dated Papa. How she listened to all the little stories the ladies told each other about the Austrian emperor's court.

But these days Opa kept busy with the administration of a very fancy apartment house. It had an even fancier elevator that I just loved to ride up and down. He doted on me since I was the first and only grandchild he ever knew. Whenever I came to see him he delighted to see how I would manage to get him to go to the sweet shop with me. And invariably I was successful. I believe the day I brought him the picture magazine and pointed to a woman in it while I, seemingly amused, said that I felt she looked remarkably like the woman at the sweet shop, took the cake so to speak. We immediately went and got some of the wonderful goodies that to this day are my favorites. Nut tortes and Sachertortes and cream-filled eclairs, and plain old chocolate-filled wafers. With things like that to eat, no wonder the Austrians were a jolly bunch!

Opa had a big Austrian Franz-Joseph mustache and a deep belly laugh that made everyone happy. He had been a widower, and Oma was his second wife. She was a very beautiful woman and I remember her being very proper. Just before my little brother was born, my Opa died. I was nine years old when I last saw him in the hospital. He was thin and sad-looking, and I was introduced to life and death. I never had the feeling that it was something horrible, only sad for me. I missed my Opa.

I never met Mama's mother and father. They had died before I was born. To make up for that, she had a very large family. Mama was the oldest of eight children. She had been kind of a mother to the three youngest ones because both her parents died at a very young age.

There was Aunt Mitzi whose husband owned a restaurant. I still remember her running back and forth in her family restaurant, with a wispy little curl hanging into her face, on a hot summer evening. She was a hard worker.

There was Aunt Liesl who had married a government official. They had their living quarters in a wing of the former emperor's palace in the heart of Vienna. It was in her and Uncle Edi's apartment we watched Hitler march into Vienna.

Then there was Aunt Katy, who had married a Jewish man. The only reason they did not get in trouble with the Nazi Regime was that her husband, Herr Adler, had left her and fled into Switzerland while there was still time. Their daughter was and still is my favorite cousin. Her name was Johanna. Johanna was not allowed to go to the Gymnasium or the University because of her Jewish father, and so she lived with us for about a year when my mother recuperated from surgery. It was either take a position as household help or be sent to some work camp. She was a household help, mostly on paper! We had fun.

There was also Aunt Mimie, who had "married into money." They lived out "in the country" in a beautiful home. Unfortunately her husband did not want any contact with any of her relatives. The only time I remember being at her house was when I was still small. While there in her kitchen, I burned myself on her new kitchen stove that had a smooth round burner. I could not tell that it was hot. I had never seen one like it. Then there were Mama's brothers Leopold, Franz, and Johannes.

Now, Uncle Poldi, as we called uncle Leopold, went on regular vacations! With a tour! I remember him as being the most sophisticated of the bunch. He had thick round glasses on his nose, and it always seemed as if he stared at one. The poor soul was almost blind! He had married a very beautiful but very mean woman and I always kind of felt sorry for him.

The next in line was Uncle Franz, who was a gifted musician. He played the cello with the Vienna Philharmonic Orchestra. He always managed to get us into the Redoutensaal when they had the first big dance of the season. There we were able to watch from the balcony as the dancers turned round and round with the old familiar sounds of the Vienna waltzes. This was the dance where the debutantes were introduced to society and I would watch how their white ball gowns swirled. I would dream of dances and gowns and being grown up! Only the dreams of dances never came true and being grown up was different than I had dreamed.

And then there was Uncle Johannes, or "Hans" as I called him. He lived with us and was my absolute favorite. He would sit in the sitting room of my home, playing the guitar and singing old folk songs. I loved him. He always had time for me, he played games with me and had the most interesting stories to tell of pirates and gold and princes, and he always knew the appropriate songs to sing, which he made up as he went along, strumming his guitar. He was Mama's youngest brother, and one day, just a day or so before the war ended, he met up with a Russian soldier. The soldier saw his uniform and presumed there was a weapon.

The soldier panicked and shot Uncle Hans—as it turned out he had no weapon. Again I met with death in one I loved.

I also had some chosen "Aunts" and "Uncles." They were friends of my parents, and we always were taught to call friends of the family Uncle and Aunt. It was not proper to address them in a familiar way and yet it would have been an insult to call them Mr. or Mrs. So-and-So. Uncle Loisi and Aunt Elisabeth had a daughter the same age as I who went to school with me and always felt she had to be in rivalry with me. I could never quite understand why. In later years I had other friends, and she remained very much a loner, with a great musical talent. She studied music and performed often in concerts, but somehow I remember that there was no life to the sound. Just wonderful technical skills. When she was 35 years old and the mother of a little girl, she died of cancer. A life spent with little joy and many anxieties. I often think of her, her ambitions, her successes, and her emptiness. How sad.

Other people wove their life in and out of the fabric of my being, enriching it by my observing and experiencing relationships.

Chicago, December 1998

Where am I at home? There used to be a place where we all were content and safe. Now, I am afraid. The children and I have no place to live. I make too much money to qualify for aid and not enough to continue to pay the rent for the miserable flat we used to live in. And my husband? Oh, how I yearn to see him again. But it will be a while before he will be released. How I hate the demon, called alcohol, that has destroyed our family!

CHAPTER 5

Family

HOME: WHERE IS IT?
As I am writing this, I am pondering what home means to me. When I visited the United States on missionary furloughs and spent time with family and friends, there were two or three places that were "home". But as the time drew near to return to Europe, I was going "home" to the little apartment where I returned after trips in the East and ministering to people in general. I was grateful for it. Its peace, order, cozy feeling to contemplate the world around me. This was "home" in Europe, and when I am in the United States with my children, that is "home." My home is neither here nor there; I find that I am a sojourner in a foreign land no matter where I am. My home actually is in heaven.

All my earlier life I can only remember "home" to be a place where my loved ones were; where security was, even in the darkest hours. Home was always a place that you came back to. No matter where you had been. A place where people were glad to see you again and accepted you for who you are. Home to me was many different places and funnily enough, none of them seem to me to have been happier than others.

Only the homes in my adult life took on different places of importance in my life. For instance, the one where I raised my own family carries with it very happy memories, even though I experienced in it the deepest level of need and sorrow, of rejection and despair. In it I also experienced the highest joys of the Lord and of human love. And so it seems that the balance of all of these experiences made it a happy home for me. But let me continue telling you of the places that were "home" for us.

First, I remember the home on the periphery of the city of Vienna. The home with the nice gardens around it. It was a two-story house made of stuccoed bricks. There were wrought-iron decorations at the windows. The house was a soft white with dark green doors. On the doors there gleamed brass keyholes and a doorbell, a brass mailbox and brass door handles, and a peephole. To keep all that brass shining clean was my job as long as I can think back. My room was on the second floor, and from it I could see the mountains and the Vienna Woods that surround Vienna. On one mountain was the tower of a radio station. Many times I sat in my big bentwood rocker, wondering who the listeners were that heard the broadcasts of the radio station. I wondered how far away the programs were heard and how it would be to see these different places.

It seemed I always wondered: How was it that some people were always sad and others were always happy.... Where would I be in a few years?...Would I be happy or sad?...

I could also see some of the lights of the city from my window. How they twinkled! And I wondered who the people were that lived behind the lighted windows. Right through the center of the city flowed a big, lazy river that was supposed to be blue all the time, it was even called the "Blue Danube". It came out of the earth in the Black Forest in Germany, and it flowed into the Black Sea way on the other side of Europe.

The second "home" in Vienna I remember is the one we moved to after being bombed out during the war. This home was closer in toward the center of the city. Very nicely located near schools, theaters, concert halls, parks, railway stations, and streetcar lines. We were located in what was commonly called Embassy Row, Prinz Eugen Street in the fourth district of Vienna. I would see the most interesting people coming in and out of the different Embassies. Black men in flowing garb, men from India with turbans, red-haired Scots, and black-eyed Italians. Beautiful women with saris and some with the sign of their caste on their forehead. People with earrings in their noses! And on and on I observed and my fantasy, already awakened by my father's reading of books to the family, got almost carried away.

Right across from the apartment house where I lived were the large and formal gardens of the Palais Belvedere, once the home of Prinz Eugen, the conqueror of the Turks at the battle of

Vienna many years ago. To this day he is a hero to many of the Austrian people.

To us children it meant one thing: it was fun to play hide-and-seek underneath the squarely cut boxwood hedges. Among our favorite games were cowboys and Indians, of cops and robbers. I remember having to scatter at times because the garden keeper did not approve of this type of activity in his domain.

This apartment was a ten-minute ride on the streetcar from the Wiener Oper (the opera house) from concert halls, from ice skating palaces, and tennis courts. It was close to all the historical places in Vienna. I loved it there.

Vienna is a very large city, windy and cold in the winter and very warm in the summer. We had the most beautiful springs with wild daffodils blooming in the parks and wild crocuses sticking their heads out of the snow early in the year. The autumn days were usually sunny and pleasant with crystal blue skies. As the shadows grew longer during the afternoon, one could discern the slightly chillier air moving in from the far mountains that already had snowcapped peaks.

Of course, nothing is really very far away in Austria. It is a small country, and our Lord blessed it with almost every terrain imaginable. From the plain "tundra-like" country bordering Hungary in the east to the majesty of the Alps in the west and southwest, bordering Italy, Germany, and Switzerland. From the big city to the smallest hamlets. From dark green forests to slow-flowing rivers. From lush green, flower-filled meadows and fields with grazing animals to the merry dancing waters of high waterfalls and foaming wild streams.

Most people in Austria are very friendly, as a rule very polished in the big city and a bit more rough around the edges in the country. But there was no such commitment to each other as I have found in the United States, unless of course people were friends. One has to remember that many wars had been fought on their soil, and there had always been a distancing because of it. Most people were nominally cooperating to stay alive. Furthermore, the time in history that this story tells was by no way conducive to trusting one another.

To sow discord, that too was the plan of the hungry spirit-bird. Nevertheless: I was at home here.

Sofia, Bulgaria, August 1999

What is wrong with me? Why am I hated? I am just a kid! I want to learn like all the other Bulgarian kids do. In a real school! But there is no way. I have no clothes to wear to school. I have no money to buy my supplies. My family thinks it is useless. People think we are worthless. It hurts. I am ten years old and I don't know how to read and write. And even if I did read and write, every school I go to for enrollment, they would send me away! They would say, "We are all filled up." So what shall I do? It isn't right that they all hate and fear us just because we are Gypsies. I don't want to steal from people; I want to learn and have a job like some of the other young people I know. I don't know where to turn. I am so confused....

CHAPTER 6

Banners and a Spirit

THAT SUMMER THE ACTIVITIES around the schoolyard were frantic. Sports happenings followed Hitler Youth camp gatherings with huge campfires. German folk songs, radio broadcasts of the speeches of Hitler and other "heroes," wake-up calls with songs, bugles, and small banners. Marching, marching, marching; singing, singing, singing; bugle calls after the setting of the sun with no one being aware that when "day is done, God is nigh." Instead the Führer saw to it that all was well....It was a very confusing time for young minds and teenage emotions.

Not many people saw what was happening to the country's children. I did not. I was impressed with all the pageantry and the friendships around the ever-present campfire and the talk of the purity of the Aryan race. Was this not enough for a young person to be proud of? Were we not the elite?

Much to my consternation and irritation, my mother played down all the exciting tales I came home from school with. As far as she was concerned, in a few years all this would not be very important to me, and she told me so. Why did she of all people discourage something I enjoyed? In spite of my feelings, she was able to rekindle in me the yearning for knowledge and the big world out there, somewhere, even though at times it seemed far away.

This was the first time that I felt a strange confusion, knowing that my parents loved me and did not want me to get all caught up in this exciting new life and yet strangely drawn to all the stirring new ideas and convictions.

Many years later, I would recognize that it was not ideas but, the spirit itself that drew me. The spirit of lawlessness, lying spirits, the spirit of fear...the Antichrist spirit. This evil spirit had marked me and thousands of other young people for a devastating fall—but God had other plans for me.

Where were all the sane people? The thinkers and the peace-loving people who believed in equality and fairness?

It seems that the whole world had their plans mapped out, including Hitler. Folks like us were mere puppets, rooks on the chess board of the world.

That fall in Munich, Chamberlain agreed at the Four Power Conference to grant to Hitler's Germany the Sudetenland (certain areas of Czechoslovakia), where a large number of German-speaking people lived. "Give Hitler the Sudetenland," indeed! Did he and all the others who had part in this own that part of a country? There were no Czechs at the Four Power Conference to object. And much like at the takeover of Austria, there was a strong threat of armed force.

On the very same day, while the whole affair was covered over with the wonderful words of "a gesture of peace in our time," British authorities handed out air raid gas masks!

On October 5 the Sudetenland became part of the German Reich. Attached to this was the promise that the rest of Czechoslovakia would be protected from any unprovoked attack. Officially Czechoslovakia was now called "The Protektorat" (the protected country). Protected from what?

Only six months later, on March 15, the "Protected Country," Czechoslovakia, was taken over by the German armed forces in a totally bloodless and unprovoked attack. The year was 1939. The bloodbath came not too much later to this small country in the heart of Europe. It was, like Austria, a corridor to the East.

Next, England signed a mutual aid treaty with Poland. Shortly after that, Hitler and Mussolini signed a pact that created an "invincible bloc." They were united with the goal to reorganize Europe. Reorganize indeed!

At the end of August, Germany and Russia joined forces in a treaty where East met West.

The left wing and the right wing of the Antichrist Spirit joined forces against the middle. Crush them. This was the blood-thirsty vulture's design, but God....Under a threatening sky and a rolling thunder, like the endless music for marching, Europe mobilized for war.

New York, August 1999

Soon school will start, and I hate the thought of it! My shoes are too small; my clothes are worn out. All except the warm jacket I found in the dumpster, when I tried to find something to eat. How I hate to do that, but I am hungry. My old lady has to have her cocaine—fat chance I will get something to eat! Sometimes I feel like I want to join her when she does her thing. Maybe it would stop the pain and end the frustration. I hate my life; I even hate myself. How would it be to put an end to it all? Would it solve my problems? Oh God I wish I knew....

CHAPTER 7

The Ugly Black Vulture

MY SCHOOL STARTED IN SEPTEMBER, and a sadness came over our class because we realized that this was the last year we would spend with each other. Some of us would go on to a school of higher learning, some of us would go into an apprenticeship to learn a trade. Our very kind and able schoolteacher, who had followed us since the first grade and had never allowed us undisciplined behavior, would stay behind to teach yet another group of pupils.

Everyone has at least one teacher he never forgets. For me this teacher was Miss Ullman. She was a spinster. She wore mostly dark clothing and always had a jeweled choker fitting tightly around her neck. It made her look very strict. Her black full apron had a sheen to it. It was impeccably pressed! We had sort of a uniform by wearing the same kind of apron. Her shiny black hair, which had a few gray wisps through it, was always neatly pulled back into a knot at the back of her neck. She had kind brown eyes that were always able to see the humor in a situation, and yet I remember them almost sparking when she was angry.

She was tough but fair and taught us some very important traits. When we were called on in the classroom to answer a question, she always gave us much time to formulate the right answer. When we did answer, there was invariably the question: On what do you base this answer? Talk about thinking! We would miss her, and she would miss us, but we would never forget the things she taught us. They would help us make decisions. We respected her.

Something else happened in September: On September 1, 1939, Italy declared its neutrality.

Did you hear the flapping sound of the great big all-encompassing wings? Or was it tires slapping against the pavement? Is the sound of metal grinding a faraway train coming to a sudden stop, or is it the war machine set into motion?

In the early dawn the sounds of metal grinding on the roadbeds at the Eastern border of Germany must have awakened many people with a foreboding of things to come. German tanks crossed the border of Poland and, in a thirty-day-long unprovoked surprise attack, Germany, joined by Russia, squeezed the life out of an ill-prepared country. It was over for them on the seventeenth day of the month. The two victors divided the spoil—Poland. In 1945, there was to be another division of this area that is still having an effect on Germany. Part of Germany would be given to Poland to make up for the part that was taken at the beginning of the war. How ravenous was the appetite of the vulture

And now it seemed like a big ball had begun to roll downhill: On September 5, 1939, the United States declared its neutrality.

On September 30, 1939, Britain and France declared war on Germany. The speed with which all these developments happened was breathtaking. It was as if we went to bed one evening free and woke up the next morning trapped.

Hitler spoke of peace plans, but all along he planned war. The twenty-fifth day of October, 1939, was a sad day for me. My Papa was called back into the service as an officer of the German Luftwaffe. Papa had been a second lieutenant when World War I ended. He was called back in his old rank and sent to Poland. There he saw a totally destroyed Warsaw and many other things that would stay with him for the rest of his life. Only once did he talk about the burnt-out buildings of the Warsaw ghetto. I remember hearing a shaking of his voice that betrayed his emotions.

There were a small group in the country who had access to "der Führer." Some of them despised what was happening and as a result an attempt on Hitler's life was made in Munich—the first. It was a failure.

The Christmas season came. Many fathers, brothers, husbands, and sons would not be home. Some would never be back;

some would be back at another Christmas. My Papa came home for a few days and I noticed, for the first time in my life, that he looked older than he had before. Frankly, I had never noticed before how old or young he was. Our small, precious family traditions were observed as well as possible.

> *That Christmas there was an ominous feeling of doom that spread its ugly wings over us like a great big, black bird and no one knew where and how it would settle.*

But life goes on and soon, the first daffodils showed their heads through the snow. Snowdrops and hyacinths reached up to the warm sun and spring came to the lovely mountains and streams of Austria.

Two days before my tenth birthday, Mussolini and Hitler met and agreed to join forces with Russia to aim at a "New Order in Europe," as spirit called to spirit. The year was 1940.

Relentlessly, the appetite of the vulture grew.

And on the ninth of April, the black bird flapped its wings again. Scandinavia: Occupation of Denmark, Norway declared war on Germany.

And once more, the hungry creature landed: The Low Countries: Blitzkrieg. Holland and Belgium surrendered to the Nazis.

To us children, as we heard the news on the radio or saw it on a movie screen, it was all very confusing. All the things we had learned about Europe and its people no longer applied. Who was whose friend or foe? Who could be trusted? We did not quite understand the enormity of what was happening to the world around us. Yet we knew we were effected by it! Just when one had made up one's mind that black was black, Herr Hitler would make a speech and appeal to the emotions, and one was not so sure any more! When one talks about Fatherland and Honor and Providence one could not be all wrong! Or could one?

Winston Churchill became prime minister of England. Shortly thereafter: Dunkirk—the successful evacuation of British troops from France. It was made necessary by the surrender of King Leopold's (Belgian) troops to Hitler's Army, which left a hole in the Allied defenses. Later, Mr. Churchill would call this impossible task a miracle of deliverance. One short ray of hope in a dark time.

And we saw it: the black spirit bird grew stronger and stronger with every harrowing newscast from the front line.

German troops marched into the capital of France: Paris. In Compiegne, France and Germany signed the armistice.

For the first time, the Germans bombed London. In retribution, the city of Berlin was bombed by the English. This would be repeated over and over, all over Germany, Austria, and the United Kingdom, from now on.

Our lives were forever altered.

Was that a hoarse cackling laugh? Or was it the sound of the anti-aircraft guns? It was the black bird's destructive force to kill and maim—but God had other plans.

Moscow, Russia, 1999

For a while we had this outrageous hope. Things are going to get better. We are going to be free to make our own decisions. The people in the West will help us with our infrastructure. And they did. But what happened? I see them on the streets—mere children. They have no place to live. I see them bonding together. Instead of going to school, they have begun to sniff glue, to take drugs. Is there no way out? There is that certain smell of poverty all around them and even more penetrating the stench of fear.

CHAPTER 8

The Claws Tighten

IN SEPTEMBER OF 1940, I entered the Gymnasium of the Humanities, a prep school, entered in Austria and Germany by students aspiring to continue their education at the university level., Before I was admitted, however, I had to pass a rigorous test and prove to be a member of the German Hitler Youth. The decision to abide by this stipulation was one my parents made with a heavy heart, I am sure. But I became a part of the crowd.

In this new school, I met many of my lifelong friends and some I have lost track of. Amongst them was Lissy Seyss-Inquart, who was a very good athlete. She and I became friends through different sports activities. Later her father was among the nine who were hanged after the Nürnberg trial in 1945. It was he who was the Minister of the Interior in 1938, when Hitler first entered Austria. I am amazed, as I look back at that time in my life. We, as young women, never bothered to find out what our friends' fathers did or what anybody believed. We simply pursued our interests and lived life as fully as we could, in spite of food rations, an absence of McDonald's, lack of clothing in the stores, blackouts, etc.

A year later in 1941, at my eleventh birthday, German troops were fighting in Africa under General Erwin Rommel; Yugoslavia surrendered to the Axis troops. Greece capitulated to Hitler's troops, and in spite of the treaty between the two countries, Germany invaded Russia on the twentieth of June, 1941.

This time the claws of the big black vulture took on a task that was to destroy it some years later.

It was also the year when Germany passed a law that all Jews, six years old and older, must wear the star of David to identify them. There was one of my classmates that did not come back to school again. A Jewish child who would not, and of course could not, join the Hitler youth and therefore was not eligible to go to high school.

My cousin Hansi could not finish her studies. She was by this time a junior in high school. All this was enacted to further control the populace. No one was to move without permission of the authorities. No one was to trust anyone else. This truth was driven home to us over and over again as our parents carefully monitored the conversation around the dinner table. There it was again: cold fear.

It was also the well-known winter of 1941, when the elements stopped the German invasion of Russia better than any weapon could. It was so cold that winter that it even made an impact on me as a child. Normally, I do not recall much about the weather in my youth. You went outside when the sun was out or when it rained. You just wore a raincoat in the rain. Simple! But that winter we all froze, even in our warmest clothing. I can only begin to imagine how the men on the front line must have felt, out in the elements day and night without shelter.

On December 7, 1941, Japan bombed Pearl Harbor. With it came the declaration of war on Japan, Germany, and Italy by the United States.

As 1942 was welcomed into history, the spirit of destruction had gathered another year of strengthening, giving birth to the "Final Solution." Men, women, and children, called subhuman, were rounded up and deposited into camps, where they worked at hard labor or were killed like cattle: Jews, foreigners, political undesirables. Some served a guinea pigs for experimentation; some died of starvation; some died of disease. They were German citizens. As far as they were concerned, that gave them safety: they died of a broken heart. The Hangman: Reinhard Heydrich.

Did you know that vultures are enticed by the blood of the weak and dying victims? The real weak victims were the Jews. The claws had tightened.

Los Angeles, 1998

We are on our way back to Mexico. I don't know if I am glad to come every year or if I hate it. It is hard work out in the fields. Just once I wish I could be in the same place for two years. Just as I get to know some of the kids, we have to move on. But I understand; it has to be that way. We have to eat. The last place we stayed at was really nice. The farmer next to the big barracks where we lived was very kind. He had nice children. One of them gave little Pepito a wonderful tricycle. I can still see his little face light up when they handed it to him. I hope there is a place where he can ride it in the next town we are in. Maybe we will be back in this area next year. I hope so.

CHAPTER 9

Sadness and Confusion

Early that fall we had moved to Olomouce in Czechoslovakia, where my Papa, as chemist, was in charge of a gasoline depot storing fuel for the Luftwaffe. He was stationed there at a relatively safe location. So for the first time we were able to live somewhere near my father. In fact we lived right on the depot property. I had missed Papa very much during the war years. I wondered how long we could stay there. Everyone was moving here and there all the time.

I remember our home there as being bright with light-colored modern furniture. I also remember a long, straight road leading to town. The road was lined with cherry trees. We children used to climb into the trees and pick cherries for Mama after we had our fill of them. Papa surprised me with a "new" fire-engine red bike. He had fixed and painted it for my arrival. What fun it was to ride down the steep hill, past the cherry trees. At times one of the trees mesmerized me and caused me to take a giant spill off my bike.

Nearby was the most wonderfully cool and quiet forest. There blueberries and other wild berries grew. Everywhere you looked you could see flowers in the semidarkness of the forest. Tall blue akelei; bright yellow buttercups; the most beautiful wild hyacinth and the famous fingerhut. It was poisonous but used to make medicines. It seemed a haven from what was happening outside. Many times I would pick flowers and bring them home to the dinner table, home where the family was. And in the winter there were the most slippery hills to use for sledding. The big hill stopped practically at our back door, where Mama invariably waited with some cookies and hot tea.

I went to school in town along with German and Czech children. I learned the language somewhat, enough to translate for my mother. At times she had a hard time understanding the cleaning woman. Mama had had surgery earlier that year and was given the authorization to have help in the house. This "help" came in the form of my cousin Hansi, who, being half Jewish, might otherwise have had to do forced labor at some farmhouse somewhere. She never felt like she was household help, but outsiders were told she was there to work. Who knows what might have happened to her had she not been with us?

Hansi was a stunningly beautiful young woman with lovely reddish-brown hair. Her eyes flashed and her tall frame was noticed by many of Papa's soldiers as she moved about our home. For me it was just fun to have my cousin living with us. She was the older sister I would have liked to have. She was seven years my senior. Hansi married, and both she and her husband became physicians. Her husband was the heir to a very large international business, and so she never really practiced medicine. She had two children. Her husband became ill with diabetes and subsequently went blind. A very sad life.

During the year I went to school in Czechoslovakia I made new friends. I remember two girls in particular. One was a very good looking dark-haired girl by the name of Hera. I always thought that this Greek name was very befitting for her looks. The other was a blonde bubble-head with long curly pigtails by the name of—what else?—Heidi! And since I wore pigtails also, I always envied her locks. My hair was as straight as that of an Indian. The three of us went sledding and skiing together and stayed at each other's homes. I suppose this was the forerunner of a slumber party. Years later after the war, I thought about them and have tried to get in touch with them, to no avail. They were German. The retribution of the Czechs toward Germans, after the war, was fierce.

And the war went on. As the troops retreated from Russia towards the "Fatherland," I saw the confusion, the total breakdown of society. I began to think about the Family Liebel from next door in Vienna. Where were they?

Their grandson Fritz had grown up with me. What had happened to him? Papa had helped Fritz get out of Vienna after the Gestapo took his Jewish grandparents away. I remember the night he came to hide in our home.

It was in the middle of the night. The rain had been falling steadily, and when one looked out the window the eerie shine of the wet pavement reflected many things. There was a moon in the first quarter high in the sky intensifying the sights and reflections of what seemed evil shadows in the darkened street. No street light was on because of the danger of bombing attacks. Across the street someone just exited the building by the light of a flashlight, and the steady steps of the person united with the drip, drip, drip falling off the roof above me. I shuddered. I remember climbing into my bed, hoping to be able to spend the rest of the night in it instead of the fallout basement. The wind blew a soft whistle against the tree in front of the window as if to say, "Close your window and go rest in peace." And so I did.

Some time later—maybe an hour or two—I awoke with a jolt. A vehicle had come to a full stop in front of the house, it seemed. Tires skidded on the wet pavement; brakes screeched. The sound of boots on cobblestones, running, stopping at the next building, followed by pounding on the door. A soft scream, shouting, someone crying. A door slammed shut; shuffling of feet; then suddenly a motor started and careened out of the street below. Where to I did not know.

I remember shaking with cold fear of the unknown. Then there was a sound much more timid then the one I had just heard. It was insistent, urgent, and frightened. It was Fritz.

Somehow he had been able to hide himself in the dark house next door and when it was safe he came out seeking refuge in my home.

What happened then I was only vaguely aware of because my Papa who just "happened" to be home for a few days acted very swiftly, and the less we all knew, the better off we were.

How he must have felt, not knowing where the rest of his family was. Today I know that his grandmother and grandfather died in Auschwitz. Today I also know that he survived the terrible war on a farm way up in the mountains where people did not ask much about the whereabouts of others. He now lives with his wife and sons in Bavaria in a beautiful old town called Landshut.

How long would this terrible war go on and on? With bombs and fires burning that no one could stop because bombs would burst into flames when they hit. People received burns on their bodies from them; some died from them. Some of the bombs made an adult person shrink to the size of a little child. It was absolutely horrible.

And how paradoxical! The newsreels in the movies showed victory and singing and bombings and more victories. Yet at the railroad stations one could see men coming home from the front lines, weary, tired, discouraged. I was confused, and many ideas and ideals crumbled, as did the many buildings and historical landmarks I knew. This too was the plan of the ugly black vulture.

As the year 1943 began, Roosevelt, De Gaulle and Churchill held a war council in Casablanca to decide the direction of the war against Hitler's Germany. This would change my life also. I lived in Gross-Deutschland (Greater Germany) and would be caught in the trap that had been set by an egomaniac.

By now Allied forces were in Africa. They were landing in Sicily. Rome was being bombed.

Mussolini was put under house arrest while King Victor Emmanuelle ordered Badoglio to form a new government. Otto Scorzeny airlifted Mussolini to freedom from his imprisonment high in the mountains of an "unattainable" fortress.

It is peculiar how hard it is for people to admit defeat. Even if one had nothing to do with it. It is equally peculiar how one identifies with one's country, as if it were the anchor to safety. Germans hung onto the deception that everything would be all right. In a way even I, as a child, who really had nothing to do with it, was swept away with it.

Finally the day came when we had to leave our temporary home in Olomouce and return to Vienna. It was hard to leave Papa again but it was prudent to do it. As the front was coming closer and closer to Olomouce it was not too comforting a thought to be sitting on top of a gasoline tank.

Every time we said goodbye it became harder.

Kosovo 1999
It is one of those quiet mornings. We gratefully catch our breath. Maybe the whole horror is over. There have not been any airplanes and there is no gunfire. Perhaps we all can have a peaceful day. What do I have to do anyway with all the hate that is being spouted by the news and by some of the people? Why was everyone so angry? I just want to live and raise our children. But somehow I sense it: I am caught in the conflict. There is no way out. Is there any help anywhere?

CHAPTER 10

Caught in the Conflict

Not far from Olomouce, where we had lived for a year, was a town called Lidice. It was razed in retribution for killing the European Hangman, Reinhard Heydrich. Thirteen hundred people killed, ninety-five homes bulldozed to the ground. What did we have to do with all of that? Oh, but we were part of it. Right or wrong, we were caught in the conflict! The German press didn't bring that as a particular newsworthy item.

We would not have noticed it anyway because we were occupied with a new task: how to get used to nightly bombings. All basements were equipped with shelves for children and later on adults to sleep on. European basements are as strong as the rock of Gibraltar, with walls two feet thick. There was safety there, or so we thought.

I remember the day well. It was a bright and sunny summer morning, the sound of insects hovering over summer flowers. The stillness of nature at the beginning of another day. And then there was another sound. The sound of the alarm wailing in the yet still summer air. We lived in one of the quiet suburbs of Vienna, and the foreign, threatening sound made us all jump. Even though we normally did not have to worry too much during the daytime, this was the day.

Mama had gone to the grocery store and I had charge over my little brother Helmut who was nine years my junior. We went downstairs more for fun than apprehension. We had a nice little section downstairs with a rug on the floor and games on the shelves. There were containers with emergency water, some blankets, a couple of pillows, some cans of sardines, a tin of crackers, a tin of cookies, cups, a big box of candles and some matches, some books, some playing cards, Helmut's beloved truck and my never-missing Teddy bear. Just in case we could not get out all night, there were some warm sweaters and a pair of sweats for everyone.

All of this array of things had been down there for weeks and up till now we really had not needed to avail ourselves of it. We didn't think we would need them anyhow. After all, we lived in the suburbs and most of the bombs that had fallen so far were on the railway stations and factories. By the time the bombers flew over us, it usually was all over for the bombing raid.

Later, after this bomb attack, when we lived in a room in my aunt's apartment, it would be different. There, we spent more time in the basement than anywhere else. Even though it was in a way fun for us children at first, it became old to never sleep in our beds.

However, that particular day we had heard the planes flying over us hidden in the clouds, and we were merely acknowledging their presence. Far off in the distance on the other side of the city one could hear the explosions shattering the otherwise still atmosphere. There was the cackling sounds of the machine guns and the powerful detonations of the antiaircraft guns way up in the sky. One always waited for a plane to be hit and come hurtling down to its destruction.

And then it happened: a whining sound far away, coming nearer and nearer, and then a terrible thud, followed by an explosion, that almost broke our eardrums. The next thing I saw was debris everywhere. Then there was deadly silence, broken by Helmut's screaming at the top of his lungs on the other side of the basement.

I felt the panicky feeling of wanting to get to where I sensed someone was in need, and yet I could not move to help, because I was surrounded by fallen bricks and pieces of rock. All I could do was to help soothe the boy with my voice.

Many years later I would remember this feeling, as I helped calm our daughter during the many nights when she was frightened, due to her illness. How comforting it was when peaceful sleep set in.

That day the plane that had dropped the bomb on us had apparently one bomb left on board and needed to unload it. It was not an incendiary bomb but it made a direct hit. It came through the attic, the second story, and part of the first floor before it burst. There was debris everywhere. We were trapped and could do nothing but wait till someone would dig us out. The feeling of helplessness was overwhelming.

   I cannot begin to imagine how my mother felt when she returned home to find a pile of rubble. She knew her children were in the house. Then we heard the noise of digging and people calling our names, and they heard our screams as well. Three hours later we began to see the light of day again and came out of the building. It was a sight that still haunts me some times. Our piano hung in the tree; all the feather comforters had burst open and there was a layer of white feathers all over the garden as if it had just snowed; silver, Oriental rugs, household goods, clothing, a fur coat, some furniture, linens, all filled the yard in various states of disrepair. Most regrettable was the loss of irreplaceable pictures and memorabilia. In short, Mama had lost everything with which she had lovingly made a home. I know she was very thankful that her children were safe.

   Part of our house was still standing but dangerous to go into. There was no organized effort on anyone's part to ensure that no one got hurt by entering the building. You see, there were too many houses like ours in the city of Vienna that had been bombed out. The work to search for the remainder of one's possessions had to be done in a hurry. One never knew when the next alarm would sound for people to flee into someone's basement. There was one thing about the people of Vienna at that time. They helped each other. So Mama and I, with some of the neighbors, dug through the remains of the house. Someone brought us boxes and we piled everything we could find that was still useful into them. Nobody had a car because of gasoline rations. So we had to go by streetcar to take everything to my aunt's apartment where we would live for the next few months.

   Neither Helmut nor I was examined by a doctor after the bombing incident. I cannot remember that we were physically hurt in any way. My brother, who was very small at the time, cannot remember the incident. Today one would be treated by a trauma expert for the damage that might have been done to our psyche. Then it was simply the thing that happens during and in the aftermath of a war. Sad, but real. I remember having sort of a hollow feeling in the pit of my stomach. That is all. But God is good and has made us in such a way that we cannot remember everything that gives us too much pain. In my makeshift bed I remember thinking that night how we had been spared. Was this a coincidence or was this my first of many encounters with a God whom I did not really know?

Will they ever stop? The sirens at night, the sound of an approaching train—much like a tornado—and the horrible thud followed by the explosions. Over and over again. Will we ever be able to sleep quietly in our beds without interruptions. I feel like a deer desperately trying to escape the hunting dogs and the bullet. It would be so easy to give into a feeling of hopelessness. But we cannot do that. Keep on going....Tomorrow will be a better day!

CHAPTER 11

Leaving Familiar Places

IT WAS SEPTEMBER 1943. The bombing still went on nightly. Authorities had evacuated the schoolchildren from the cities, so that they had a more normal schooling experience. My school was evacuated to Slovakia, near the city of Bratislava, not too far from the Austrian border. Mama and Helmut were sent to a town on the Czech border called Laa/Thaya. It didn't seem to make any sense, but then nothing made much sense. No one had a choice where they were sent; where they went to school; what happened to them. We had lost control over our lives a long, long time ago.

One morning I remember being evacuated, leaving my mother and brother. I had a pair of skis, a suitcase of clothing, and a rucksack with my schoolbooks. There were hundreds of children at the station. Each had a tag hanging around his neck with his name, address and school on it. The destination on the identification tag sounded very far away. All around me families hurriedly hugged and kissed goodbye as if to push out of their thoughts the pain of separation. Pain was written in their faces. Fear of the unknown future. There were some tears. Mama and I too said our farewells.

As the train moved out of the West Station in Vienna and Mama and Helmut became smaller and smaller, I learned to let go. I can remember crying in the bathroom, so no one would see it, as I wondered if I would ever see them again. I was thirteen years old.

It was such a relief *not* to hear the sirens, or the whirring sound, or the thudding of the hits followed by an explosion, that we almost became thankful to be away from our families. Soon after our arrival, life became a routine of sorts. We all learned to arise by ourselves at a given time and to share all things with each other—toothpaste and soap and especially cookies and other delicacies like dried apples and apricots sent to us by our families. And sometimes we found things missing without being shared. We also found good friends who, like us, were homesick, and we comforted each other. We learned caring for one another. We learned about life.

But that did not mean that the avalanche that had been started by one Herr Hitler was no longer in motion. Quite the contrary; lulled into a quiet security, the day came when, like a bomb, it hit us again.

I believe the hardest thing to learn for me was the fact that I had no way to contact my family, except through official channels. Not all official channels were sympathetic to the feelings of young girls and boys under these circumstances. We never knew if everyone was well at "home," and the mail did its best to get through, literally, while the bombs fell on the railway stations.

Time did not stand still as we began to feel the weight of knowing and seeing more than our years should permit.

I did not know it, but as my birthday drew near, Hungary's Jews were being sent to Auschwitz while the German troops withdrew from the approaching Russian forces. When it became evident that our safety was at stake, the same German troops took us into their tanks and on their trucks and transported us to Vienna.

I never thought I would like the feeling of being in a tank churning away in the direction of home! Oh, I might like the excitement of it in normal times; but this was not a normal time. And yet I was glad to get into the churning steel horse that moved slowly and constantly toward home. The deafening noise mattered little to us. We hoped to see our families soon. We gladly left some of our belongings behind. Even my Teddy bear, which I had smuggled into my gear. Home. How would it look? I shook at the thought.

When we arrived in Vienna, with thousands of other children, we were immediately taken to the Westbahnhof where we were loaded into trains going to wherever our families where. In my case I got a new tag with my name and destination around my neck. My new destination was Laa/Thaya, and I was loaded on a train going toward Czechoslovakia.

To describe the noise and confusion at the railroad station is hard to do. Names were being called as children went front and center; some cried loudly; others had silent tears running down their cheeks as they stoically stared into space waiting for their turn to come. "Just get us out of there and 'home,'" I am sure was on everyone's mind. Frankly, I have no idea how in the world they kept track of who went where. But I suppose that was part of the German efficiency one reads about. Lissy and I parted when we came back from Slovakia that day. I went to be with my mother and brother. I remember her being picked up by a big German limousine. There was a last wave of farewell to my good friend. The next time I thought of her was when I had heard of her father's incarceration and the trial at Nürnberg.

It was essential that we leave immediately. Vienna was now being bombed both day and night. The Russians by day and the English and American planes by night. Continuously, demoralizingly, dangerously spreading death all around.

Would there ever again be a time of leisure; of safety; of deciding for oneself what one wanted to do? Who were these enemies? The Russians and the Americans? I did not know any of them and yet they ruled my life. What was wrong with my own country? Why was the deception carefully veiled so as to insure our cooperation. Since when did we have to be afraid of things, day and night?

Many years later I would find not only a new home in America, but subsequently help Russian Christians struggling for freedom. What the enemy of the souls of men meant for destruction, God redeemed.

Pristina, Kosovo, 1998

I saw them coming. It was as if a bright, sunny day all of a sudden turned gray and hopeless. I have never seen so many hollow-eyed people hanging onto what is most important to them. For everyone it was something different! Children mostly and old forlorn people seemed important. But then there was the one that had a small tractor. Or the woman desperately coaxing her old and weary goat up the steep path. No matter how you looked at it, it was a mass of humanity lost in a strange land. How would all this end?

CHAPTER 12

The Nightmare

THE HAMLET MY FAMILY AND I WERE SENT TO was Hevlin, Czechoslovakia. It was located just across the border from Austria. In fact, while I went to school there, I crossed the Thaya river, which was the border, on a bridge every morning and evening.

This small farming village took their produce to the somewhat larger market in Laa which was in Austria. Hevlin consisted of a long street with houses on both sides. There was a town square in the middle. On it was the mayor's office, the church, a bakery, a butcher, and a general store. All the fields were outside the village, and every morning the farmers would go to their fields with their oxen and equipment. Taking their equipment was easy. They still cut the hay with a scythe. The whole household would move out to the field every morning.

The oldest woman would stay behind, cook the noon meal for the farmer and the field hands, and take it out to the field at noon. They stopped to eat only and then immediately continued their work. It was not uncommon for some of the pregnant women to have their babies in the morning and be out in the field in the afternoon. They were a tough breed of people.

The only place Mama was able to find for us to live was an old farm house that nobody had lived in for several years. I can imagine how hard she had to work to make it look at least somewhat inviting for us. By the time I got there Helmut and Mama had been there for about two or three months. It was a typical old house with the attached stable on one side and the barn on the other side. There was no inside bathroom. The old outhouse was out back. We had a bathtub that was brought out once a week for the traditional Saturday night bath with water heated on the stove. The rest of the time we just washed up with a washrag, and our hair was washed once a week. Of course small children would have been bathed daily in a small tub.

There was a large kitchen with a wood-burning stove. It was also used as our heat source during cooler days. We had two small bedrooms. The sitting room got its heat in the winter from the tile wall that formed one side of the kitchen stove. Around this tile wall was a bench. It was ever so cozy to sit on it and lean against the tile wall on a cold day. It was not very luxurious but we were together.

It was difficult to make friends there in this environment. Basically, we did not "belong." We were city folks. For my brother Helmut and me it was not too bad. We always found someone who wanted to go swimming in the river or play ball with us after school. But poor Mama had not a soul that she could have fellowship with. People also were suspicious of anyone they did not know. Too many people all of a sudden disappeared in the night. Papa was still somewhere in the service. The mail had long ago stopped to function very regularly. It must have been lonely for Mama.

What had happened to the "Thousand-Year Reich"? It was as if people wanted so badly to have nothing happen to them; or perhaps that they could not face the fact that they had been lied to, defrauded by their leadership. They still listened to the radio reports; cheered with the newspapers at the glowing reports of "Victory" while their cities were in ruins and their animals were dead. Their men were either killed or already in POW camps. They saw the twelve- and thirteen-year-old boys and the sixty- to eighty-year-old men called to duty. Yes, they gave the young boys guns to shoot with, if they were available. Others were arming themselves with sticks and stones.

Even when the people from the Balkan countries came with their few possessions they dismissed it. These Balkan people must be low-class folk. This certainly would never happen to them! The depth of the deception was so great that there were still people going to meetings where they yelled "Sieg, Heil" (Hail, Victory) and raised their right hand as if to greet a god.

The horror of the unending columns of fleeing people, driven by one enemy from behind, met by the enemy before them, crushed between two warring spirits never became real to me until many years later. We were so busy surviving.

Yet, for some time now we had noticed larger crowds of people than normal coming through the village, pulling little wagons that seemed to have all their earthly belongings on them. Every so often some goats would pull some of them or even a cow. But one thing all of them had in common: they were gray-looking, tired, weary, and hungry. And one more thing: they all had sort of a hunted look about them that made you shudder.

Mama made a decision: we would dig a huge hole in the backyard and lower into it a strong wooden box lined with tarpaulin fabric of an old tent. Whatever was left of our earthly belongings—Oriental rugs, silver, china, glassware, paintings—we would store in there. We then would bury it in the soil. We would take with us only those things that could easily be carried in a suitcase. And we would take advantage of the offer of the German army who would take civilians anywhere on their own route. Mama wanted to try to get back to Vienna. One could beautifully disappear in the city where millions of people lived. This was also where my Papa might be looking for us when he got back from wherever the war had taken him. By now victory did not look too promising.

So we took care of all the things concerning our household goods, and then we made ready to go with the next caravan of trucks going in the direction of Vienna. Little did we know that the next few weeks would put us into a position of being tested almost beyond our human capacities. Neither did any of us comprehend the strength, power, endurance and wish to survive that God puts into all of us when we are born. "I knew you in your mother's womb..." For me personally it would prove to me, once and for all, that the God of the little Catechism book of the Catholic church was alive! He was listening. He was faithful!

There was some sort of foreknowledge of things to come. That strange feeling that one can expect situations that are totally foreign and will require special attention. I could not put my finger on it, and I did not discuss it with anyone, least of all my mother, who had her hands full of getting things in order. She tended to last-minute details.

We took some food with us that could be eaten without cooking it. Salami that would not spoil; boiled eggs that would keep; bread that would soon be hard. Apples, pears, a jar of canned pork, some cream of wheat and oatmeal; thermos bottles with hot tea and coffee and some water. All these things were in small amounts and were stored with Mama and Helmut on the first truck designated for women with small children to accommodate them with a possible supply of milk on the road. The rest of the people found their own places on the vehicles. I was on the last truck with Mitzi and Franzl, two young people my own age who went to school with me.

Mama had fixed us a last bowl of potato soup with some sausage in it before we left that evening. In fact I remember munching on some apples as we made the last preparations. To tell you the truth, that is one of the few times I remember eating in the next three weeks. I am sure we did have something to eat at times but it was not as important to us as surviving physically, and so I can't remember.

In hindsight I wonder how Mama felt: leaving everything she still owned of worldly goods behind her. This was the second time for her. Leaving a roof over her and her children's heads; moving from the place where my father had left us. And now again a move. Surely this would be the last one! I am certain she knew much more about the fate of the refugees that had come through the little town than we did. But she kept it to herself lest she frighten me.

Mama made sure I had on clean clothes that were warm. I remember putting on my woolen skirt and a sweater over my blouse. My knee-high socks, strong hiking shoes, and my green Loden coat and hat completed my travel outfit. Most of our luggage was on the truck with her. All I had was my rucksack and my accordion.

It was pitch-dark outside, and an icy-cold drizzle made traveling very uncomfortable. Off we went on this cold and rainy night. Night travel was considered safer because of the constant vigil of the Russian fighters. Oh, how the minutes ticked away! At first we tried to sing, and then, one by one, the voices stopped and we were left alone with our own thoughts.

All went well until all of a sudden our vehicle sputtered and shuddered as if under a great strain, and then it stopped totally without another sound. The men tried very hard to get the vehicle fixed, for they also needed it to get where they were going. But to no avail. We were the last truck in the caravan, and it was hours before anyone in front of us noticed that they were missing one vehicle. Being a mother, I dare not even think how my very own mother must have felt when she realized what had happened.

It meant that I would have to walk to Vienna, because the trains had long ceased to run and besides were far too dangerous for a girl by herself. We found more people who had the same destination and so we began a long, long walk home to Vienna that would prove to be life-changing for us.

My friends, Mitzi and her twin brother Franzl, and I were all of a sudden aware of the fact that decision making concerning our survival was in our hands. I was fifteen years old and so were they.

Soon we ran into some folks who had fled the Russians. This time the stories they told us were very frightening. Of shootings and of women disappearing, of starvation, a lack of water, and for the first time we heard of the supposed safety in the western part of Austria. There, the more civilized, or so it seemed to us, Western Allied troops were in charge.

So we made a decision. In order to be safe temporarily, we would take the long way to the western part of Austria. Much later I would learn a lesson from this. What seemed a safer thing turned out to be just longer, not safer. Had we gone straight to Vienna, we would have had much of the trip behind us while we were still hiding in holes in the ground.

*It seemed as if somewhere in the depth of the shadows that surrounded us there was the sound of laughter that made your blood run cold. A glee at having won a battle in our life. But **God** in His mercy allows us mistakes and upholds us with His strong arm.*

Oh, what a cold early spring it was as I and thousands from all different parts of Europe moved about the roads. People went from place to place to find families, existence, places to work and live, to hide from authorities. Some gained from other people's miseries, some let fear reign in their life. Others showed mercy and kindness. A few greedily picked up suitcases that we had discarded only a few kilometers back because it was not important enough to have the contents if it meant sapping one's strength. At times I felt real empathy with the little rabbits running from the foxes.

I noticed as we walked along, during some of the moonlit nights, that there were definite telltale signs of a war all around us. We had to watch the deep craters made by bomb or artillery hits that had filled with the water of the melting snow. The sun was now much stronger during the daytime hours, giving us welcome warmth after many a cold night. There was a sadness over the entire land as if the earth itself grieved about the deep trenches made by men for their defense, about the furrows cut across acres and acres of land by tanks rushing to their destinations.

The breathless waiting for green shoots bursting through the fertile topsoil was marred this year. There was no grain peeking through the brown soil. No corn and few potatoes making their appearance in the warming spring sun, for you see, there had been no one to plant the seed. The roads we followed went through fields ready for the farmer's hand. They had not been worked yet. But the land was always there. A hope for the future.

Many wells that had supplied the water for the farms for watering their cattle and horses were putrid with the stench of death. Dead animals had been thrown down into the water holes to force the inhabitants of the land to capitulate if the fight went on too long. But it never came to an extended fight to the end. The farmers were weary; the people in the villages were tired. They were frightened; they were saddened and confused. There was much suffering because of it. There was no clean water to be had in many hamlets except the small creeks that came bouncing out of the mountains.

And the mountains! Ever beautiful. A quiet manifestation of the power of our Lord's creation. They were too tough to be damaged by this war; instead they hid a lot of secrets of men and women moving from place to place. There, they were hidden, inaccessible by the sheer height of the towering rocks. It would be so easy to get lost forever in the world of eternal ice. Many frightened people did. This land, which became something special to all who walked it during those memorable months, had a peculiar strength to it.

Even the lovely valleys, displaying the first signs of spring like a promise of a future to come, seemed strong. The fresh green of the Austrian larch trees, in the middle of a forest of darker firs and pines, greeted the hiker. Tree-lined roads served to protect animal-drawn carriages from the hot sun in the summer and the blizzard winds in the winter. They were the calling card of this part of the continent, much as the white birch trees were in Siberia. When we were younger, we climbed them and hid behind them during our summer vacations.

But in the spring of 1945 they served to hide us up in the branches and to be a guiding marker for our weary bodies. We knew if we followed the line of trees we would undoubtedly get to the next village or town. In the past these little roads had had a nice smooth roadbed, but the inescapable war machine had churned away at it; by now they were hardly more than dirt roads. While we slept in the daytime there was a lot of activity on the roads. Often we would be awakened by the rumble and shaking of the earth by an oncoming caravan of military vehicles. But at night when we traveled it was just us and the stars and the moon above.

We came across civilians who were fleeing from somewhere to somewhere. It really did not matter where as long as it was safe. Of course there were others who had the same destination as we did and who could be trusted. And so I learned about discerning. We three young people were bound together. There is nothing so binding as the combined effort at survival, which is God's greatest natural gift to man. From the day that we decided to be a team, we separated ourselves from the rest of the crowd, because we observed that a large crowd could be very dangerous. It drew the attention of fighter planes that were constantly striving the roads. And to this day I have a scar to prove it. A bullet that bounced off some rock. It also drew the attention of

Russians who had been promised by their officers that if they won the war they could have *all* the spoils of war they desired. Their desire put us in jeopardy.

We tried eating unripe apples, with devastating effects; we tried to find potatoes, but they were not quite ripe yet. But there was always grass. When we found an empty metal can we were joyous, because now we could cook something, if we had matches and something to cook. Some kindhearted soul gave us a small box of matches. When we found a small cave-like ditch under a bridge we set out to find clean-looking grass plus some water from a brook, and presto! grass soup it was. What can I say? It was warm, it filled a big hole in our stomachs, and the little fire, which we built just before dark, kept us warm for a few minutes, and that felt good.

Surely this nightmare would end some day; would we ever again have a real meal at a real table with our families or would we find out that we were all alone in this world? Oh, God, please help us.

Kosovo, 1999
I wonder how many people there are in this area? Once it was a meadow, now it only looks like a mud hole. Perhaps tomorrow they will have a few more tents to protect us from the rain. I really don't feel so safe in this place. But it is better than where we came from. There is a little water, and they say it is safe to drink. It is so discouraging to be told to do this and that and to never be able to make any move on your own. We have no rights here. Oh, I know they try to do the best they can for us. But we are without rights....

CHAPTER 13

The Granite Building

FINALLY! THIS IS EXACTLY HOW WE FELT: we felt safe to drink the water, we were under a roof, this was better than some of the places we had been and put our head down at night. The Austrian authority told us exactly what the rules were, and it seemed all right. Then why did we feel so uneasy about the refugee camp in the big granite building? Did it have something to do with the foreboding I had felt some time back?

We had walked a long time. We were tired, and we thought we were going in the proper direction to get to Vienna. It was clammy cold and wet. Our resolve gave way to a feeling of being driven. Then, out of nowhere some German army vehicles offered us a ride. Oh, how good it was to sit down and not have the rain pour down on you! The benches were not too comfortable in the truck and when our eyes got accustomed to the dark in the truck we realized that there were others in the truck who also were on their way to somewhere. Where? No one knew. But we did not realize this truck took us on a much more westerly route than the road we had taken before. Actually much more west than we had wanted to go. The distance between Laa/Thaya and Freistadt is 100 miles. We did not arrive at our destination during the night. It was daytime before we arrived in town and were dropped off.

Only then did we realize that these soldiers were fleeing the enemy they had fought for weeks and months and wanted to take a chance, even an uncertain chance, with the Americans. They were headed for the zone in the western part of Austria. We still had much territory to cover. It was still a long way from Vienna.

No one was thinking of sleep; yet we needed sleep because we were exhausted. By now I had learned to sleep in any position necessary, on any surface available, in light or darkness. No problem! We noticed that there was a refugee camp in the big granite building, and since we did not have any money, this is where we went.

The building was an old government building that had been used as a Kaserne for the military. There were three floors and an attic. Pretty large building. We were told to go into the attic area, where there were no beds. But somebody had piled straw to be used as pallets. Perhaps it was the most uncomfortable accommodation in the building, but, as we would soon find out, the safest. The toilets were on the floor below, and there was good drinking water down there also. A toilet and drinking water! What a blessing! Oh, perhaps we could even wash out some clothing! But before we ever got to that point we fell asleep. We slept soundly during that day and through the next night.

At dawn we were called downstairs to the courtyard, and it was at that time that we noticed that we no longer had Germans but Americans that were giving the orders! I listened intently. For the first time in my life I was thankful for my Welsh English teacher, who very strictly enforced the rule that all people were to speak English in her classroom.

That morning we had the first solid food in a long time: good old dried eggs and milk and stale bread, some raisins, some corn flakes (only at that time we had no idea what those were), and plenty of chewing gum. Oh, it was delightful, but we could not eat a whole lot; we were full quickly.

Someone asked for an interpreter. I timidly raised my hand and translated the best I could what was being said: The Americans were going to retreat beyond the Enns River to give the territory over to the Russian forces according to the treaty signed by the victors of the war. We rejoiced! The war must be over! Wonderful, we could finally all go home! But it would take a while longer. Little did we know that our real test of survival was just beginning.

We were offered an opportunity to be taken to the U.S. Zone of Austria. In other words, all who wanted to go to the western part of Austria could be transported by these American forces as far as Linz, Austria. Well, that was not something we wanted!

After all, we wanted to get back to Vienna! And so we planned to get some more rest and then set out again on our trek.

The Americans pulled out that very morning. It became very still all of a sudden. Eerie! Like a vacuum. It seemed as if a dragon of doom were about to strike. For a brief moment I regretted not having gone with the Americans, but soon we entertained the more pleasant thoughts of being home with our loved ones. The daylight faded. Slowly night fell. That is when we heard the familiar sounds of grinding tank treads coming to a full stop on the pavement in the street below. Then there was shouting and the splashing of water in the water trough in the courtyard below. There was laughing and burping and obscene noises coming from below. We all had the same uneasy feeling: we had made a mistake. We should have left when we could. Oh, God, what would this night bring?

We went out the attic door and peeked down the stairwell. All we could hear was a conversation between the soldiers and the Austrian officials. It would remain quiet until the full cover of night had set in. Then we heard it: the unmistakable language spoken by Russian soldiers who had begun to celebrate.

Austrian officials trying to stop the men, who began to push into the house and up the stairs, had no chance to do their job. We heard a loud slap and then a thud. Our protector had fallen.

Then there was more noise from the second floor where a very unfortunate woman was caught by them. We could hear her screams as they dragged her into a room...

We feverishly disappeared under the piles of straw. Small children sat on us. Baggage was piled on us. We had the uneasy feeling that our life was out of our control. It was in the hands of others. If the Russians were coming to get us, they might or might not find us, depending on what some of the people in the attic said. We knew that we would have to get out of there, and quickly. We also knew it would not be very easy. There was a guard on duty at the bottom of the stairs who monitored all coming and going.

Have you ever smelled fear? We did. Bone-chillingly so.

Eventually the Russians did make their way up the attic stairs. They did find a poor woman, dragged her into the dimly lit hallway, then raped her right in front of everybody, including her husband. The man wanted to help his wife. He was first hit and, when he did not give up the fight, he was shot in cold blood. When the woman finally was able to get up, she screamed like a wounded animal. I will never forget the screams.

I honestly have no idea what happened to the body of the man, nor how or when the Russians left. I felt like being dead. I did not move. It was something we observed from our hiding place and it traumatized us. Honestly, at that moment all I wanted to do was to get out of there Later, I tried to shut the whole episode out of my memory. The only thing I remember is that when you are in a refugee camp you are at the mercy of whoever is in charge. I never wanted that to happen again.

That very night we moved downstairs as quietly as we could. When we had come to the second floor we climbed out of the window and carefully let ourselves down to the ground. Of course, this meant that now we had nothing but our little box of matches, which had become very important to us. As we moved through the dark night, fearfully ducking into the shadows, we swore to stay together and always be there to help each other.

We always tried to hide wherever we could, especially when it rained, and, as I recall, it was a very rainy spring. Sometimes we found folks who gladly let us stay in their stables or in their barns; then again we found folks who for a loaf of bread or a box of cigarettes would tell Russian soldiers where we were, and we would have to hide quickly. One night we had to climb out on the roof of the barn in order to get away from our pursuers.

One morning, after walking all night, we were bone weary, hungry, and thirsty. We threw caution to the wind and asked to stay in a farmer's barn. We were even brave enough to ask for not only water but also food. They laughed at us. Food! Who had any? But they did allow us to get water from the well, and they let us wash our hands and faces. Oh, it felt so good. We even played with the thought of rinsing out some of our things, but we had no soap, and we feared not being able to leave at the drop of a hat if we did that. We forgot about it. We slept peacefully all day, and when night came and it still rained, we toyed with the idea and finally decided to stay for a while longer. Just till the rain stopped!

I don't know how long it was, but suddenly we heard the sounds of a truck approaching. As we listened we heard loud Russian talk that came out of inebriated mouths. They were obviously looking for something. We did not take the time for long guessing games. We began to dig into the haystack as fast as we could. Then we remained as silent as possible. We were so glad it was pitch-dark in the old barn without electric lights. The men were very drunk.

Here was this thought again in my head. Jesus. Was He really alive? Trustworthy? People talked about him. I remembered how he performed miracles in my old Bible storybook. I did not have much time to get into a soul-searching debate with myself. All I could do was to send up a prayer: God, if you really are up there, directing people's lives, as I have been told, now is the time that you might show yourself and help us here, or we will die. Nothing was said aloud—only in my very heart and head—and yet what followed would be encouraging to me all my days, it would be proof of God's salvation power in the world for me, and it would serve to encourage other people as well. Finally God's response itself saved our three lives.

I remember shaking so hard and hearing my beating heart so loudly that I felt sure I would be found out. Holding our breath, we waited. And they came. I could smell their sweaty bodies and their breath of alcohol. Are you going to let me die here, Jesus? I thought. I have no idea how long the ordeal of waiting was or how I got through it. It seemed as if I was in a bubble, protected by...whom I did not know.

Trying to find us, the soldiers stuck their rifles with fixed bayonets into the hay. One bayonet cut my shin. Neither he nor I noticed it. After they left, I realized that there was a huge cut on my shin and the blood poured out profusely. I had not felt it, nor had I made a single sound.

The men were angry because fifteen-year-old Mitzi and I, the women promised them, were simply not there!! With much cursing and loud shouting, they left the barn. We were safe. God had proved Himself to be alive. As I look back on the incident, I am not sure that it made any particular impact on me at that moment. I know that it helped to shape and form me into what I am today. We were simply glad to be alive and took off under the cover of the night, rain or no rain.

One day, or should I say one very early morning, just as daylight broke, we traveled on a road that we knew led toward the suburbs of Vienna. In all the days we had traveled together—and it had been almost four weeks—we had never found one Russian soldier who would prove himself to be helpful or even polite. On that particular morning, at a Y in the road, as we debated which way to turn, out of nowhere appeared a Russian officer who was all by himself. In very good German he warned us not to go on the road we had decided on. To take the right side of the Y. All three of us had heard and seen the man. We stopped in our tracks, looked at each other, and debated, but when Franzl turned back to respond, there was not one person to be found anywhere. We were shocked, to say the least, but we headed into the direction suggested by the officer, which proved to be our salvation.

There was even a neat little ravine, hidden by some bushes under the overpass, that we could clearly see in the light of the rising sun. The man had pointed in that direction. Had we gone the other way, we would have fallen into the hands of a caravan of Russian trucks filled with victorious soldiers.

At the time we did not think too much about it, because there was so little time to think about anything. But since then I have had time to reflect. First, where did the man come from? There was no vehicle anywhere to be seen, no town close by, no house around. Second, No Russian officer at that time in history traveled alone without a driver or someone else with him. He had the shiniest boots on in spite of the dusty roads. He had a marvelous dress uniform on. And he looked nothing like the short, swarthy looking horse-riding fighting troops we had seen. He was tall, blond, blue-eyed and spoke impeccable German! How did he get here? The whole thing was like an experience moving in slow motion before our eyes.

Today I believe it had been an angel in disguise to watch over me. The most awesome thing is, that I had not received salvation at that time, but God knew me, he knew my heart, and he knew every hair on my head, my needs, my weaknesses and my strengths, but most of all He knew my yearning, yet unknown to me, and how I would respond when the time came....

Kosovo, 1999

I have never felt such a roller-coaster of emotions in such a short time…our anticipation turned into fear, which became horror as we viewed the things happening before our own eyes. And yet we were grateful because we were still alive but there was this incredible sadness that came over me as I looked around and I saw all the suffering humanity in a state of shock. Again there was this foreboding of a future so uncertain it made me cringe. Oh, how would it go on? Where would my children ever find a home again? Is there even a chance that we will find my husband? How I long to lean on his strength. I am so tired.…

CHAPTER 14

Coming Home

WE WALKED AND WALKED for what seemed to be endless hours. Finally we came closer to Vienna. I became excited as we saw the houses in the distance. We looked again and realized that all the houses were bombed out. In the early-morning hours, before the sun had penetrated the canyons of the city, the buildings resembled sad faces with hollow eyes and gaping mouths as if screaming out in pain. We understood. At this moment we felt the same way. We were bone-tired. Too weary to care and yet longing for safety.

We had seen a lot of destruction during the past years, but this was different. It was quiet in those dawn hours, there was no sound of rushing bombs, yet the enormity of the destruction we witnessed was overwhelming. We too felt like crying out in pain. What had happened to our homes? Would they be like this? The smoking rubble of a once-beloved haven full of life and love? Was all the former life gone forever? Would there ever be security and beauty again?

We did not know it, but a whole country, more so, a continent was silently asking the same questions. It would be many years before this nightmare would be eradicated out of the lives and memory of the people.

There was another fact that became clear to us almost immediately: every bridge across the Danube River was blown up except one. That one, the Reichs-Brücke, was manned by Russians who were checking the identity cards of everyone attempting to pass over the bridge. We did not have identity cards; we were not old enough.

How would we manage? What could we do? Did we dare to cross over the river on the bridge? What would they say when we told them we had no ID? Would they believe that we were only fifteen years old? All three of us looked tired, dirty, and older than our fifteen years. Franz might get through all right, but Mitzi and I were very much in danger.

In the past, while hiding, we had witnessed the taking of young and old women. Where to? We did not know; but they never came back again. Might they be dead or might they be somewhere in Siberia? Always they were taken, supposedly to perform work, in kitchens, cleaning houses...who knew?

I, for one, would not take this chance. The other two joined me in the decision. We had come this far, we would not fail to reunite with our families, nor take the chance of being abused or even killed. We decided to swim the mighty Danube River under the cover of the night and hold onto each other so we could help each other if need be.

I believe again at this point God's wonderful gift of preserving self from destruction took over, and led us to make decisions far beyond our years. They were executed the following night.

The hours between dawn and that afternoon seemed endless. Hidden behind some bushes so as not to draw too much attention to ourselves, we looked at each other: filthy, dirty, with torn clothing, skinny, with every bone showing through the sleeves of what had been new not too long ago. We were mere caricatures of ourselves, and we seriously began to wonder if anyone in his right mind would even recognize us at all. Our shoes had long been "repaired" with cardboard from a box we found on some trash heap

That day we saw and heard what we had feared might happen to us. Many people, especially women, were searched, questioned, and then taken away. And we wondered where they took these women? We saw fear loom over all that went on, like the ugly demon it is. God protected us supernaturally; nobody saw us. Eagerly we awaited the night, to put our plan into action.

As darkness and fog set over the Danube River, we began to rip a shirt and with it tie one to the other, so we would not lose each other as we entered the ice-cold river to swim across. Many thoughts went through my head.

We will surely die in this icy river. Who knows how fast the river is flowing in the middle? What if a large steamship comes along and we cannot get out of the way fast enough? What if one of us gets a cramp or does not swim well enough? What if they catch us anyway—over on the other side? Oh, it would be so much warmer to come back out and go over the bridge! The voice of doom and discouragement, that does not belong to God, was there badgering us. We risked the task that seemed impossible: we went into deeper water. Is this the end? Will we make it? The river was very swift, and we could tell that we were floating somewhat downriver. All the adrenaline that our young bodies possessed was utilized, and, wonder of wonders, Mitzi first found footing in the mud of the riverbed some three kilometers down stream. We were jubilant, after swimming and swimming without seeing where we were.

It is impossible to describe the coldness in our bones. There was not one dry thread of clothing on our bodies. The frigid air coming out of the hills and mountains, with patches of snow in the hollows, went right through us. This was something we had experienced before, but not as intensely as now. God in His goodness kept us safe and warm in His hand.

Exhausted we fell under the next bush and huddled together in the cold of the night. There was no sense in moving just now. We had found out that the four occupation forces that ruled the city of Vienna were enforcing a curfew from sundown to sunup. So finally, we began to relax a little, and as the warmth that the swimming activity had produced gave way to chattering of our teeth, we noticed something.

There were light beams moving over the water, back and forth. How extraordinary that none of these light beams, which were obviously there to prevent people from doing what we had just accomplished, had noticed the three bodies moving through the dark water. Was this another one of the "coincidences" that had happened to us in the last weeks?

The people of Vienna were a people occupied by four forces: American, British, French, and Russian. It was best to stay hidden. We also knew that the next morning brought to an end, at least temporarily, a friendship upon which our lives had depended for weeks. We had built a trust that led us to victory over life's strange developments. And so I learned about trust and friendship.

For a last time we kept each other warm under the cover of darkness. The river rushed along tirelessly toward the east, never stopping, always moving. Would we be the same way? Would we find a place where we again rested and felt secure? Eagerly we awaited the first rays of the sun to warm us. We were ready to move on into an unknown future.

I wondered why I was here, half frozen, bothered with all sorts of conditions I had never before encountered. Because of the lack of water and facilities for bathing, we were dirty, full of lice. We were bitten by fleas from sleeping in hay. If we were sick, we didn't know it. We had not taken the time to pursue the possibility. My hair was matted down. Starved to a mere ninety or so pounds, hungry and thirsty, with my heart pounding in my chest, I wondered: Why was I alive? Would the sun ever rise again? Would I ever seem normal again? Where were my loved ones? Would they recognize me if I did find them. Were they still alive? Oh God, *help!*

But the sun did rise that morning, and, being young, we were rested. We picked ourselves up and started up the embankment of the great River Danube. As we reached the Kai Strasse above, with all the bombed-out buildings looming over it, we had to make certain decisions again. My home was toward the west and theirs toward the east. And so for the first time in weeks, we parted company. With promises to see each other soon, we prepared to go home. Home!? How wonderful that sounded!

I longed for the warmth and closeness of a family, or someone! Some being that was full of strength. Where I could be safe. Where I did not have to make decisions any more, that would either keep me alive or be the cause for my death. There was an incredible loneliness. Paralyzing. But God knew the outcome of this feeble beginning. He knew the prayer of a mother that penetrated the damp, cold darkness, pleading for her child. In my loneliness and exhaustion, God was there.

Would I be able to find my family? Were they still alive? Dear God, why did life have to be so hard, so complicated? I literally felt a peace set upon me, and, with a sense of security that I did not understand, I set out to find my loved ones.

It was early that morning, before the sun was up. A few kilometers from where I was, my mother was awakened. In spite of curfews and dangers, being a woman by herself, she set out, driven toward the River Danube. She would later say that she did not really understand why she went. Or why she went that morning. She followed an inner impulse that somehow gave her hope.

Near the spot where we had come up from the river was a street. It turned south from the Kai Strasse. Everything was full of debris. The whole neighborhood could not be recognized because the whole street was a skeleton of partial buildings. The exposed rooms gaped like big caves, with no place to hide any life beyond. Determined to find my way, I turned the corner to proceed home.

Oh, how the wind blew that morning. It blew dust and bits of stone and ashes everywhere. It took me by surprise. As I lifted my eyes to search straight ahead for familiar sights, I could not believe what I saw in front of me. Afraid to have been a victim of an illusion, I closed my eyes tightly and then squinted. There she was! I walked almost straight into the arms of my mother. It is impossible for me to describe the feelings that flooded me, as I saw her. Joy, relief, unbelief, surprise: it all culminated in many tears.

To this day, I cannot understand how my mother recognized me. I had lost so much weight. When this long march started I had a little knapsack with a toothbrush, a comb, a piece of soap, a heel of bread, a small bottle of water, and one change of underclothing in it. On one of our escape maneuvers, we even had to drop our knapsacks in order to get away. In the weeks that we traveled I washed completely maybe three times. Otherwise we just dabbed at our faces. Somehow we managed to keep the small water bottle and whenever we came to a creek we filled it. The creek water was safer to drink than water the many polluted wells produced.

I must have looked like Cinderella right out of the ashes. My shoes no longer had any soles; instead the soles in them looked like on a piece of Swiss cheese, they had been "repaired"! Here I was, a mere caricature of myself, but a mother's eye sees through the outer shell. Poor Mama! She was thin and worried-looking, and there was a haunted look on her face. I later found out that, while she was at one of the refugee camps, she was raped by several drunk Russian soldiers. When I heard that I did not ask anything. I would not have known what to ask, nor did Mama want to talk about it. Now I know that on Mama's mind was the big question: Had I been spared? After making sure I was fine, we moved on. We did not want to draw undue attention to ourselves. We proceeded toward the place that my mother had found to live in. It was given by a kindly woman in our old neighborhood. It was a haven of security for us, at least for the time being, until my father could be found.

I didn't wonder how and why my mother came to this precise spot in a city of several million people. I was just glad she had. It was not until much later that the thoughts came: How did my mother know to come to this precise spot along the Danube? Of course, this was the only place people could come across, the only bridge still standing. But why on that one particular morning? As I thought and thought about those things, I could not find any reasonable answers. Coincidence? Enough to leave my sleeping brother behind? The boy was asleep when we got to the quarters.

My silent question had been: did God really care? Now, I began to see God's hand in it. Again, God knew me, my heart, my desires, my fears, my hopes. And I began to desire to know Him also.

Skopje, Macedonia,1999
After all these weeks I hoped to find my husband. The refugee camp! The stories that circulate: I hear they killed 43 men yesterday...really? Some of them the Serbs took prisoner. You know what that means! Where did that happen? I am not sure...Oh, God let me not listen to all this. I would rather continue to hope to find Sergey. The children are becoming frightened. I must find a way to stop all of this useless chatter! In my heart I know we will find him!

CHAPTER 15

The Search

ALL THAT WAS ABLE TO MOVE ABOUT IN VIENNA in the next weeks was the well-known Jeeps of the four occupation forces. These four-wheel-drive vehicles were able to plow through all the debris. There were no other vehicles. I often wondered what happened to people who had to be rushed to the hospital. Was there even a hospital that one could rush to? I really don't know.

The search for my father took us all over Vienna. But we were not the only ones doing this. There were wandering people everywhere. Some were finding shelter in bombed-out buildings, under staircases that were left intact, in entryways of houses. Mama made the sign of the cross on our foreheads; then she would go in one direction checking the doorways, and I would go in another direction. We went daily to look at the thousands of small pieces of paper that could be found in doorways, nailed to doors and walls:

> If anyone knows the whereabouts of my
> husband Walter, last seen on
> November 14, 1944 at Baden bei Wien,
> please let us know...mother, wife, etc.

> Or: I am looking for my husband Herman
> shown on this old picture.
> I have found a place to live at Rennweg
> 18, Wien III.

I can still see the heavy, carved oak doorway on a busy intersection on the Ringstrasse. It was right across from the Opera House, next to the bombed-out shell of the former Hotel International. There was one note next to the other. People stood for a long time trying to get a glimpse of a name or an address that was familiar. Soon it was known to all seekers that there one could find loved ones who were thought to be dead or in prison camps. Many came after finding their homes destroyed by bombs, hoping against hope that their family was not in the house when it exploded.

Oh, God when will this ever end? I thought. When will the appetite of this insatiable spirit ever be satisfied? But God always triumphs over evil. He shows us small glimpses of it when we need it. I began to trust Him.

Wives were looking for their husbands. Fathers and mothers looking for their children. Friends inquiring about each other. Families desperately in fear of what might have happened to their loved ones. Hundreds of people standing at every bulletin board, in front of every large doorway, at every subway station. They were looking and crying, hoping and laughing. Many of them comforting each other. Day after day, never giving up. Please God, let this be the day when we find my Papa's message!

Every single person found or looked for had a story. Papa also had a story. After we found him, he related his story to us. My Papa had contracted malaria while he was stationed on the island of Sardinia in the Mediterranean. He was subject to renewed attacks from time to time. The end of the war found him in a prison camp in the English zone in northern Germany. It was customary, after the war, for prisoners of war to be moved from one place to another.

One day, the guards again moved some of the prisoners, and my father was one of them. He had just started with a renewed attack of malaria and told the guards that he could not move another step. A kindly Scottish sergeant warned him. He was exasperated and tried to tell Papa that they would have to shoot him if he did not move. Finally, he decided that, rather than kill my Papa, he would leave him behind. And so, after crawling into an old bombed-out building in Braunschweig and shaking with the fever for a few days, he began the long walk from northern Germany to Austria.

The first thing he had to do was to rip off any recognizable signs of his being a German officer. Off came the stars. A trade was made with someone. Riding britches against simple work pants. He had a little satchel with a razor and some underwear that had been allowed the officers in the British camp. He traded it. Somewhere near Frankfurt, a farmer gave him a shirt that did not look like a military uniform. Papa had worked for it. Around Munich, the family of one of the men in his air force outfit let him stay there for a day to rest up. He made his way without discharge papers this far. He knew that, to get across the border, he would need discharge papers from the Allied forces, which he did not have because the Scotsman left him there to die in Braunschweig. What else was there to do but to cross the mountains under the cover of the night? The mountain pass still had several feet of snow on it and, watching the guards' movements, he crossed over the so-called "green" border.

He had calculated it would take him about twenty-two minutes to come across and down past the guard shed. The changing of the guard took, as far as he could see, roughly twenty-four minutes. He waited for the German guard to be distracted by his Austrian counterpart, moved close to the shed, and, when both were in the guard shed, dashed to pass them. After crossing over to the Austrian side, he hid himself till he could see the guard, having completed his first patrol, stop to talk to the German guard. He swiftly moved downward toward home. Having taken hikes in the mountains in this area, I am fully aware how dangerous it is to move about in the mountains if you are not well equipped, especially at night. Papa surely had an angel watching over him.

One morning, as we did every day, we went to check all the entries to buildings that might have a clue to the whereabouts of my father. Often we were discouraged because we found not a trace of our Papa. But that day, as Mama crowded into the doorway with all the other searching people, she could not believe her eyes! There it was!

> Karl Krepelka. Looking for my family.
> Last seen in Olomouce. Please leave word
> with Harry, Favoritenstr. 4; 2nd floor.

The search was over! In a city of several million people, most of them moving from one place to the other, we located my father! It was a miracle like so many other things I had experienced. I found I really could look to God for answers. How strange! This was a new experience.

Joyfully we went to the given address: there was Papa! He was exhausted and thin, but he was here! With us! It took Papa a while to become himself again. I remember him more quiet than I had ever seen him. But he was alive.

But there was one loved one who was not alive to be with us again. My beloved uncle Hans. Mama always took care of her youngest brother. He not only lived with us, he was a confirmed bachelor. Once, when I asked why he had never married, Mama explained to me that, when he was younger, he had been much in love with a girl who decided to marry another man. From then on he decided to remain single. Uncle Hans was very much a loner. Our family was very important to him. He was less military-minded than anyone I have ever known. He hated guns. He worked for one of the oil companies. He was an accountant.

My school was on his way to work and so we walked together every day. And every day he handed me ten groschen for a small Bensdorp chocolate bar for my lunch. We would be chatting away about riddles and games as we walked along. He was my hero. One day, he was called into the military service. He served somewhere in an office in Germany, keeping books for the German army.

When it became apparent that the war was lost, Uncle Hans made his way back to Vienna. There, he went to our old apartment, thinking we were there. He was confronted by some Russian soldiers who had moved into our apartment. Someone saw him go up into the attic to hide for the night. The next thing that happened was very sad. Uncle Hans had no weapons on him, and yet a very anxious and panic-stricken soldier shot him in the dark of the attic. I will never forget him. I loved him.

We found out through the authorities that some of the items we saved after the bombing attack were still in our apartment where poor Uncle Hans found his death. But we had to wait until the Russians left the city, some years later, to get our belongings back. Many soldiers had stayed in our apartment; as a result many of our things left with them. Goodbye, dainty china cups, wonderfully polished silver utensils; someone else is enjoying them now. Spoils of war.

But all of that was not so important to my Papa. He somehow managed to bring things into the proper focus. He always knew what to do! We had waited for him to act on our behalf and act he did. Papa! He knew that to survive one had to have food. Food was much more plentiful in the country than in the city. He also knew from experience that when one was willing to work for it, one could be paid in food, not money. Immediately, we went on a long trek to Upper Austria which was under the command of the U.S. forces.

As we left the Russian zone and entered the American zone we were very closely scrutinized. There were lines of people who, like ourselves, moving from one place to another, waited in line to be "inspected." What this entailed became immediately clear to all of us. It meant submitting to the safety precautions and cleansing measures with DDT against any kind of unwanted crawling creatures on your body. This was a very degrading procedure. It was an especially undignified and demeaning act to be performed upon anyone who had just been cleaned up, like me! And so I began to learn that not one person in the world was able to totally control his life. For he who used the DDT on me was being yelled at by his superior, who in turn did not look too happy himself. Ergo....Oh, well.

This moving about was so unlike the people of Europe. Most of them were born in a place and died in the same place, often in the same house. Over the past few years many of us had learned to hang up our hat and call it home. These indeed were different times.

That fall, as the leaves began to turn bright orange and red and yellow, my family and I were somewhat settled in a new environment. I had never before lived on a working farm. But that is where we were.

In the summer we all went out to the fields at 5:00 a.m. and learned to cut the hay with a scythe; we learned to turn the hay to let it dry, to hoist it up to the wagon. With pitchforks we lifted it up to the loft. Nobody had machines to do the work.

When we were out in the fields at noon, the farmer's mother or wife came with a big basket of sliced farm bread and a milk can of soup for the farmhands. She brought it on a small wagon. There was a cup for each of us for the soup and a hunk of bread. After we had finished that, we could have a cup of water out of the water can we had brought with us in the morning. After we ate we went on with the work again and at 4:00 p.m. we made ready for home unless it looked like rain. In that case we had to finish, no matter how long it took. I have always appreciated the hard work of a farmer after doing that kind of work just one summer.

Papa was wise and knew that we would be better off in the country because the chances of finding nourishment would be better. I knew no one who had any money or whose money was worth anything. The banks were still closed.

People in the cities were not as fortunate. There was no food to be had in the stores from May till late September except for an occasional find after a few hours standing in line. These past years as I have seen the food lines in Moscow, and the bread lines in Romania, the hungry children in Albania, Gypsy children rummaging through garbage dumps, the picture of 1945 came back into my mind vividly.

As the first week of September came, we youngsters, for once, were eager to return to school. School was six miles from where we lived for me and about four miles for my brother. I remember the incline to the old farmhouse as being very steep and slippery in the wintertime. My brother Helmut had a particularly long walk in nasty weather or in snow, for the path led along the fields. There were no school buses. I had to walk about a mile to the next public bus stop, and, I might add, if I missed the bus at 6:30 a.m. I had to walk all the way to school. It did not happen but once or twice.

At night we all caught the only bus home for the schoolchildren. It left Wels at 5:15 at night. Then we would walk home from the bus. We studied for the next day one or all of the fourteen subjects, gratefully ate our dinner, and went to bed. There were no times for real fun during the week, except on the bus and during our lunch hour, spent at the park in the warm weather or at some inn during the wet and cold days. There were no cafeterias or study halls. But we managed, and life became a serious conquest at a very early age.

Mama had been asked to help in the big farm kitchen where they fed thirty working people every day. In exchange for it, we had food. Another reward was that we all were able to live in our little "apartment." The farmer had taken one of their old hay barns and converted it to emergency shelters for families. Our "apartment" consisted of one room with two beds in it. The bedsteads were filled with straw mattresses. Whatever wearable clothing we had was hung in our "closet"—the frame of the door into the next "apartment." We all had a stove in it for cooking and heating and a table to eat on. Period. Water was downstairs at the well. The toilet was an outhouse behind the building. It was hard to get to and freezing cold in the winter.

As primitive as this seems, it was a gift of heaven. Before this we lived in an open barn along with about thirty other people. For a whole month. No privacy. The whole scenario was a nightmare, and yet it was in this little haven of family life that we experienced the first peace and real joy for many years.

Finally it was Christmas! And the joy at being able to be with my family this year was all the gift we needed. I remember that particular Christmas as if it were yesterday. It was the clearest night I believe I had ever seen in all my life. The moon was shining brightly on the fresh fallen snow, and it glistened like a thousand stars.

Mama had saved up an egg each week for several weeks, and so we had some honest-to-goodness Christmas cookies. The smell of them baking made our mouth water and added to the joy of the night. The table was set with the finest we had. Four plates that did not match, nor did the glasses, but it was Christmas in our hearts.

After supper we children left the one room we occupied so that all the mysterious whispering could go on. Now my mother could properly prepare to display our few little treasures. A pair of new mittens, some knitted socks, a game that my Papa had made and a book with stories in it. A real book, not just one from school. We children also had gifts to give. I remember my brother had made a little basket out of willow branches and had filled it with beautiful stones he had collected in the creek bed that was located along the edge of the forest. I had unraveled a sweater that did not fit me anymore and had made some potholders. A few weeks earlier I remember Mama saying, "I cannot imagine where your yellow sweater went"!

More than any other year we had enjoyed getting ready for Christmas Eve. Together we went into the woods, cut our small tree and brought it home. We had made beautiful decorations for the tree. We had strung small pine cones and nuts. We stuck small red apples full of cloves to hang on the tree. They smelled all through the room. Somehow Papa had managed to find five candles that were burning round the little tree. And then we sang and sang, songs of joy and thanksgiving. Soon it was time to go to the midnight mass.

As we stepped outside, all bundled up, ready to walk the four miles to church, we could see them. From everywhere they came, bright lights, coming down from the mountains; and we could hear them sing, children singing everywhere. Sleigh bells ringing in the night and finally, joined by many more going to the same place we broke out in Christmas songs:

> Stille Nacht, heilige Nacht,
> alles schläft einsam wacht,
> nur das traute hoch-heilige Paar
> holder Knabe im lockigen Haar,
> schlaf in himmlischer Ruh.

> Silent night...

We entered the Village church, crowded with people who rejoiced as we did. The candles warmed the unheated church as we huddled together and the message rang clear in the winter night:

> Glory to God in the Highest and Peace on
> Earth for men of good will!

The year 1946 was ushered in with celebration and with a certain hope born out of desperation. It could only get better. What a relief it was not to feel the ever tightening claw of the horrible black bird at the back of your neck!

Every day, after school, we went into the forest and collected all the small pieces of wood we could gather and bring home with our sled. Sometimes it got dark by the time we would get home, but we knew that we needed to do that in order to stay warm and cook the little food we had. I remember longing for the first warm days, even though I soon forgot about it when I was throwing snowballs with my brother and the other children in the neighborhood. I somehow wanted to be a child once more, but I had seen a lot and lived more intensely in a short period of time. I knew nothing was ever going to be the same again for me.

So when the winter snow melted and spring started with all the flowers breaking forth out of the fertile ground, I was glad that I was allowed to go for walks like a grown-up. This gave me some time to think all the private thoughts I had in my head.

My brother saw the first bananas he had ever seen; I was able to buy a new pair of shoes. The first new shoes. I had been wearing Mama's shoes, and they were a bit snug on me. In desperation I learned to make clothes. You notice I did not say "learned to sew." I made them out of feed sacks like the frontier women, bleached in the sun and sewn by hand without a pattern. But there were no dresses in the store yet and I had outgrown everything. I had blossomed into a young lady.

Oh, but it was glorious; the day came when there actually was a movie theater that had a film to show, and down at the old inn the young people had a dance.

That March 20, 1946, I turned sixteen.

I often wondered what had happened to all the people I had encountered during the past few years. Were they as blessed as I was? Were they alive? Every once in a while, I thought of the strange life I had led so far, and I wondered how it all fit together, the puzzle. There was a vague yearning after what, I did not know. But the yearning never left me.

We swam in the lake that summer, after working in the fields, and life seemed very simple. The next year marked my last year at the Gymnasium and then—I wasn't sure. It was expensive to go to the University. We had just begun to rebuild our lives, and besides, there was my brother and it was more important for a man to have a good education.

In October I read in the paper that they had hanged the nine men that were accused at the Nürnberg trial. And I could not help but think of Lissy Seyss-Inquart. I wondered where she was. How would I feel if my father....Sometimes I didn't understand the world.

My last school year went by faster than anything I could ever remember, and the time had come for graduation.

It was June of 1947

Detroit, Michigan, 1998

Well, here I am in the Juvenile Hall. I never thought I would end up here. How did I get here anyway? I remember my old man saying, "You will end up in jail if you continue running with this crowd!" Oh, I never took him serious. But he was right. It is too late now. I remember him saying: "Discipline, that is what you need; discipline!" He was right. Perhaps I can learn to discipline myself? I do want to try!

CHAPTER 16

The Convent School

If I had no particular plans for my immediate future, my mother did. She decided for me that a young woman would have to have certain skills to prepare her for marriage, the raising of a family, cooking, sewing, etiquette, and all the things a finishing school taught.

And so I entered the convent school for young ladies. There I was painfully introduced to the fine domestic arts. It seems, somewhere during the years of the war, that subject had been neglected. In fact, the matter of personal discipline had been neglected also, since my mother had very little input, at a very important time in my life. Little did I know that I was about to enter *the* school of discipline.

The convent was about fifteen kilometers from Mauthausen, Austria's wartime concentration camp. At that camp the incarcerated were Jews, criminals, Christian leaders, and political prisoners. When the gates opened in 1945, an untold horror was witnessed by the townspeople. Mauthausen was in a valley. It was in the Russian zone of Austria. A river called the Enns flowed by the convent's high walls, which surrounded the buildings and chapel like the fortification of a castle. Inside were a beautiful garden, stables, fruit trees full of delicious fruit; the school, the living quarters of both pupils and nuns, and a lovely old church. The convent was almost totally self-supporting. We supplied the labor.

It was with apprehension that I entered into the convent school. It was with displeasure that I remembered that my loving parents, whom I had always trusted, had put me there. Some nights, awake in my bed, I even considered the options I had. I decided there were only three options. I had to make a choice. To run away was one. To cry "Help!" and let my parents get me out was another, but not a good one, for I knew I would have a hard time convincing them. And the third was to submit to the discipline of the school. I hated it at first, and yet I learned real discipline there, even more than at home. And it was in this environment—quiet, thankful, joyful, and expectant—that my Lord moved. He moved in a way that certainly was unusual and unexpected. I learned that one is able to hear the voice of God better when one is in an environment of order, cleanliness, and piety. Even though I never wanted to stay there, it was what I needed at that time in my life. It was where God wanted me to be.

I threw myself into the schoolwork and planned to excel, for it was easy compared to the scholastic requirements of the school I had just graduated from. I had learned one thing in my earlier school years: not to waste time but to learn, for what you learned could not be taken from you. I made friends with a girl by the name of Anna. She had also grown up in Vienna, and, like me, had longings she did not understand. She and I proceeded to compete in all the courses of study, not in an unpleasant way but to prove something to ourselves and to others.

And it was here that I learned about pride in my life. It became so important to have all A's and to really cook well. To really set the best table, and to really have the cleanest wash. To know how best to feed your family, to take care of little babies. It even became really important that both Anna and I do better than anyone else with the chores of a farmer's wife, who had to supervise many employees. It became so important to us that we almost missed the reason God had put us there. It was a hard lesson to learn. We ended up eating a lot of crow to show the rest of the class that even though we were from a city and not from the country like many of them, we could be their friends.

As the choir director listened to the voices of the new arrivals, I was picked to sing alto. This would prove to be a real tool of God to show me His word. I had never before read the Bible, nor did I know that all the music we sang was not only by the great composers, but it was all spiritual music. It was either out of Psalms or the Gospels or other parts of the Scripture.

Not knowing any part of Scripture, I just marveled how moved I was by what I sang. Again and again, during the parts of the mass, I saw the Jesus I had heard of in my little Catechism book. There was lots of time to ponder, during the quiet hours, when no one was allowed to speak. And it was during those hours that I knew there was something wrong with me. I now eagerly began to look forward to church. We went every day in the early morning and, of course, on Sundays and holy days.

Somehow I knew what was wrong with me had to do with what I felt when I sang the songs of adoration. My heart would beat faster in anticipation of something that was coming my way. What was it? Filled with longing, I prepared for the Easter season to come, in song and in heart.

Every year, the Mother Superior of the convent invited a Jesuit priest to come and minister for a week to the needs of sisters and students alike, in preparation for the jubilant culmination of the week before Easter. This year however, "something" happened and instead of the usual Easter visitor we saw a kindly old man, in the brown habit of the Franciscans, celebrate the first mass of the week.

As every week, all of us in the convent went to confession. We were expected to confess weekly and then take communion on Sunday morning. Which was a real source of rebellion on my part because, you see, all the sins I confessed every week and was forgiven for were repeated weekly. On top of that I had to confess weekly to a man. Not to God, to a man. Kindly though he was, my pride and exasperation at never being able to do better provoked me to rebellion against professing to a man. I ask you—who does not get angry at times or be unkind or even lie! I for one was sick of coming before God weekly with a lie on my lips. Please forgive this sin and this one, I will never do it again...and yet I did do it again. I thought one had to be good enough to be forgiven! But this was a special time. God knows the needy ones and is teacher as well as Savior.

Somehow, I felt that this was a very special time in my life. I was not sure why. I only knew that something was missing in my life. Somehow it made me angry that I could not find what I was looking for. There was no rest in my soul. No peace in my heart. But God knew...

I remember distinctly, as I entered the lovely, peaceful church, I experienced a quiet, restful atmosphere. There was an expectancy in the air. I could not put my finger on it. In the confessional a very kind voice asked about my needs. I found myself blurting out all the things that had gone through my head and heart. I told of my longing for something I did not know. I confessed that I would never come to confession again and lie to God and if this was all there was to life, who needed it! Unthinkable! In the confessional! But God...

With kindness, the Franciscan explained and explained that there was a Lord who had died on the cross for me and that if I believed this in my heart, I would live forever. I should know that there was nothing I could do to receive eternal life myself. That repentance led to forgiveness. Even the promises of never again sinning did not matter, really, that it was the blood of the Lamb that had the power over life and death. He then told me that I had to decide if I wanted to receive this everlasting life. He even promised me that as I began to walk this new walk, I would be able to withstand the temptations of life. And then he said a strange thing. Not to pray this or that prayer, but to "go and speak with God, my child." This time I wanted to take communion.

That was Good Friday, 1948.

For days I cried at the very least remembrance of Jesus. In my heart, the longing was stilled. It was this fact that told me over and over that something very wonderful had happened. Years later I would be able to reconstruct what had happened. It would be the Lord Himself showing me the date of my salvation.

The following day I walked on air. The sun seemed just a little brighter than on other days. We went to pick flowers for the Easter tables the next morning. I marveled how wonderful God had made the world, as I looked at the beautiful blossoms of the wildflowers from the field behind the convent. It had been a long time since I had noticed the bees and how they collected their honey. How each little ant carried its own load to be part of the ant community. It seemed that the humming of the flying insects and the wonderful smell that came from the earth beneath our feet, being warmed by the spring sun as it and dried out the dampness of the morning, was a newly appreciated experience.

It was then that I sang for the first time with a new joy, "The heavens declare the Glory of the Lord."

I learned many skills at the convent school: sewing, knitting, fine needlework, cooking, planning meals, setting tables, using silverware, glasses, and plates correctly, correspondence, health and child care, laundering, ironing, supervising household help, and—since many of the girls came from farms—how to take care of farm animals and to work in the fields.

Nothing was spared to smooth out the rough edges of young minds and bodies. And so I learned that work honors a person if it is honest work. As long as I live I will be able to earn a living, feeling good about it, no matter what it is.

Soon, the two years of my schooling were up, and I could finally go home. I had missed my family, only being able to see them at Easter time, Christmastime, and twice in the summer. Once, for a whole week! This taught me to become self-sufficient; later I would have to unlearn some of it. I also learned to be alone but not lonely.

My next adventure came when I was assigned to work on a working farm with one of the other students to run the household at the farm. My boss, a veterinarian whose young wife would much rather shop than work in the kitchen, was a very nice and gentle man with much patience. We proved to be efficient, and so, after three month of internship, I became an honest-to-goodness, graduate of the School of Domestic Arts for Young Ladies. My fellow student Anna remained there for several years until she married.

Next, I decided that I wanted to go back to school to learn languages so I might become an interpreter. In high school I had taken Latin, English, and German. I was proficient in German and semi-proficient in English. I wanted to become proficient in English and take Italian, French, and Spanish in college courses.

I applied for a job as nursemaid to English-speaking children and got the job. For two years I took care of the little ones, one boy two years old and one four years old; it was hard for "Maria," as they called me, to leave them when they returned to England.

Two years of speaking nothing but English, during the day and most of the evenings, sharpened my knowledge of the language. I was now ready to find a job that would not only pay me better but also give me a chance for advancement and maybe some savings to go to school as I had planned. When a job opened in the Ordnance Maintenance Accounting Section in Salzburg at the Depot I took it, hoping to be able to find a suitable apartment or room.

I was determined not to become a refugee again. How fortunate I was! At a time, when millions of displaced persons were living in refugee camps trying to find accommodations, I found a lovely furnished room. It was located right on the river Salzach, and the view out of my room was breathtaking. I could see the Untersberg towards the east gleaming in the morning sun, much as Maria in *Sound of Music* must have seen it. And when I looked toward the city, I could get a wonderful view of the towers of the many churches and behind them the majestic outline of the Fortress Hohensalzburg.

This was an exciting place for me to live in. I was now grown up and could go places. Even though Austria was still not rebuilt, musicians would play the all so familiar music of Mozart and Haydn and Bach to the joy of the listeners. The Mozarteum was filled with foreign students, and the city was coming back to its original cosmopolitan flavor.

Through renting a room in the beautiful spot in Salzburg, I got to know dear friends. They owned a house, were willing to rent me a room and to take me into their family and hearts. To this day their grandchildren tell of the times that their mother or father found me to be the only person willing to accommodate a pair of cold feet early on a winter morning.

Those were happy days; we had more sense than money but cared little about it. It could have gone on like this forever I guess, but God knows best. He knew I would need to remember my Easter experience to carry me through a life that had barely begun. I had buried the experience of one lovely Easter in 1948. Later I would have to repent for being so thankless.

Grassau, Bavaria, 1998

How come, when I think things are beginning to move ahead, there is a change? I have done a good job for the company. So why is the promotion given to Ursula? It really is not fair! Wait, when I see the boss! He will hear what I think of the whole situation. I am sort of embarrassed, too, in front of all the others. But I guess I ought to be glad because I still have a job. In this day and age jobs are not easy to find. Maybe the next time if I work hard...I mustn't give up. I can do it!

CHAPTER 17

Learning Flexibility

JUST AS I WAS BEING CONSIDERED for a good promotion, the four Allied powers made a peace treaty with Austria. Before we knew it, Austria was without an Occupation Force. I was asked to stay with the job until the very end. In return for it I was given nine months' separation pay. But no matter how one turned it, I was without a job. The Austrian authorities didn't show much concern for people who had over the last few years earned more than the average worker doing the same work. So, instead of being unemployed, I took the separation money and all the wonderful letters of recommendation I had collected over the last few years and went to Heidelberg, Germany, where a very good friend and coworker lived. She had married an American the previous year. She was glad to have me live with them for a few weeks while I made application for a job. I was told that I had to have a residence permit, and when I went to get it, they asked me for proof of a job. So it seemed hopeless.

But "hopeless" was and is not a word in my vocabulary! Being the resolute person I had become, I asked my friend's husband to speak with his boss for me regarding a job. You see, I had already applied and paid for some courses at the University. I was being interviewed by a very nice elderly lady who made a proposal to me: I could enter their Teletype Section as a "poker" provided I could learn to operate the confounded thing within three weeks. I was given permission to come and practice as many hours as I wanted and given a special pass to get by all the Military Police, since Heidelberg's Teletype Section was in the same building as the Code Section. It was the Communication Center of Headquarters United States Army Europe.

Today, you would say: "What is a teletype operator?" In this age of computers there is no such thing. Then, three weeks later

...you guessed it: enter one new teletype operator. And why not? After all, was not the Lord in charge? This is where I would meet my future husband all the way from the United States. So I went to school in the daytime and I worked at night in the Teletype Section. I don't remember sleeping, but who needed it? I was young.

The week before Thanksgiving of the year 1955, some new men arrived at the office. They seemed very forlorn, away from home at Thanksgiving time. And even though I only had a very tiny apartment (a little kitchen and a living/sleeping room, with the bathroom shared by two other tenants), I invited the three newcomers for a Thanksgiving dinner. It was not a simple thing. I could not just turn the oven on; that would have been too easy! No, one had to have the proper coins for the Automat that would provide the electricity for cooking, lights, and heat. Twice that day I ran out, and the second time I had to borrow some coins from one of my neighbors. It is particularly unfortunate if you happen to have a cake in the oven! But it did not quench the festive spirit that ruled the household that day.

Even though I had never had a Thanksgiving dinner I knew what it meant to be far away from home; and so I listened to the three fellows who were invited concerning what would be appropriate. Then I began to substitute. Turkey—scratch it—chicken instead. Sweet potatoes: not to be had in the German stores at that time—scratched—french fries instead. Green beans I was able to come up with—good. Salad I was able to come up with. Dessert was a different story. Never had I known anyone that ate pumpkin pie! But I did know how to make apple strudel. Rounded out with ice cream, which the fellows brought with them that day, we came up with a meal fit for a king. On that day some friendships were formed and one of them would bloom into love.

The year 1956 caused me to think over some serious things very carefully; for one, it became clear to me sometime during the summer that I had fallen in love with David. Someone who lived several thousand miles from where I had lived all my life. I was twenty-six years old, ready to settle down, to have a family. Up until then, I had been afraid of many things that brought back very unpleasant memories of 1945 and the long trek to Vienna. I would have nightmares for two or three years after my marriage, and only love and security and the Lord's strength helped me over all that had been.

We set in motion the wheels that were necessary to marry an American soldier. But neither David nor I knew what an exhausting job it was to be permitted to marry. The armed forces had a rigorous examination I had to endure from sergeants and commanders, physicians and intelligence. But it all came together and on the cold sunny morning of February 9, 1957, with only my family and a few very close friends present, we exchanged marriage vows in the small Army chapel. Till death do us part. I remember having no money but being happy.

We did not go on a honeymoon. Instead, we moved my few things into an apartment that could accommodate David's gear as well. The method we used to move I shall never forget and I believe is worth sharing.

After packing up all my earthly belongings in about three boxes and two suitcases with one lamp on top. We brought it all down to the streetcar stop. With me on the last platform and David following with my bicycle, we moved in a grand fashion. Today I cannot explain how we did it, but we did.

In that respect I have truly come full circle. Today I could easily pack all my belongings in just a few boxes and suitcases. It is a wonderful way to live. No maintenance. Being free.

That spring we traveled some. I was anxious to show David more of my very beautiful country. We visited my relatives and friends who all wanted to meet the new husband who would take me far away. Oh, how time flies. There was so much I wanted to do before our trip to the United States. Indeed, the time had come for David to return home. June was the magic month, but there was no magic about it to me, because I did not have my visa to enter the United States yet.

If any one thought it was hard to get the commanding officer's permission to get married, it was even more difficult to persuade the American consul general to get a entrance visa for a new bride in a hurry. Letters were sent, people called at consulates, U.S. Representatives interceded, and finally, the day before the scheduled departure, lo and behold! my visa arrived.

Right there I learned that one did not need anything until it was needed. A lesson I had to remember over and over in my life and sometimes still have to relearn. I often think of how graciously God taught me all I needed to know. He was never in a hurry; He was never late. How well He knows us. How He streamlines the learning experience to each individual.

The last day of May 1957, David and I went to the railroad station in Heidelberg. All our friends waved a last goodbye to us, as we got into the assigned sleeping compartment in the train that was to take us to Bremerhaven. There we would be put on an army transport, the *General Patton.*

The trip across the ocean was amazing to me. I was put into a cabin with other women and some children. I remember one of the women was expecting a child. She was not very well the entire time we traveled on the ocean. I felt sorry for the little ones and took them up on deck once in a while to give them a bit of fresh air.

My new husband, however, was stuck in the lowest part of the ship along with all the other soldiers. Having no children, I was scheduled to be fed with all the "married but without children" females. David, on the other hand, was on the first feeding roster, and so it came that, by the time I was fed for breakfast, he was almost ready for lunch, etc. We did have some time together, though. In the afternoon they would show a movie in the "green room". Since some of the movies were such things as *The Green Berets,* we somehow felt that it all matched our complexion. Not a good choice of a name for the lounge on an ocean ship.

At night, we would have a time together to walk on the deck designated for families. We would walk, watching the sun set on the immensely large, forever changing, sometimes smooth and sometimes angry-looking sea. Or we sat and dreamed of being in the United States. Of a job, a house, and a family. Of meeting all the folks in the U.S.A. I would remember the dear ones I had left behind. I felt lonely and yet not alone.

Oh, dear God, make it that they will like me; let me find a family like the one I had left behind.

Every night David took me back to my cabin, kissed me goodnight, and went back to his hammock buddies. Not the best kind of honeymoon, but then it only cost me $7.00 to come here to the United States! $1.00 per day. It took seven days before landing in Brooklyn, the smoothest crossing, so we were told.

Kosovo, 1999

I can't believe that it is over! Oh, how I longed for this day and yet not all is clear to me. Some of our friends have already taken off to go back home. "Home" how wonderful that sounds! But no one really knows if there is still a home. Tomorrow, just as soon as our Baba feels better we too will begin our long walk back to our home town. We have all waited for this day for a long time. We still have the land even if the house is destroyed. It is the only hope we have. Yes, there is hope. My children will have a place to grow up in. We will again have food to eat when we are hungry.

Oh, God, how will it be? Maybe I don't know you as well as I should. But please hold us in the palm of your hand. Keep my husband safe if he is still alive and protect us on our trip...

Tomorrow we leave. Tomorrow...

CHAPTER 18

America

TOMORROW WE WILL LAND. Tomorrow! The date will be June 7, 1957.

On a bright and sunny day, waiting out in New York's harbor for a docking place, was the USS *Patton*. The weather had actually been so good that we arrived in five days instead of seven. And a good thing it was. My new husband was with a few hundred other soldiers who were just as eager to get off the boat as we were. For two days and nights, while docked out in the bay, we could see the lights of the wondrous skyline of New York. The Statue of Liberty with her torch burning brightly seemed to be there welcoming all of us. During the whole last day I dreamed of what it would be like. It certainly looked nothing like any skyline I had ever seen in Europe! Then we landed.

I experienced New York like a dream. The proverbial word *greenhorn* certainly was a well-chosen one. Never had I seen anything so large. The buildings, the avenues, the crowds, all were oversized as I saw them for the first time. I never, ever, had experienced such bright lights at night as when we were walking toward Times Square. Little wonder that all I could remember were the blackouts in Europe during the war and the cities slowly being rebuilt. The shop windows fascinated me. I was thrilled to see Tiffany's and some of the sights I had heard about but never dreamed I would actually stand in front of. It was 1957, and it was not too dangerous to walk the avenues at night and window-shop.

I was almost sure the people in Brooklyn didn't even speak English. The hotel we were taken to in large buses by the Army was in the heart of Brooklyn. I found it hard to understand some of the conversations going on around me. There was a window in our hotel room, where I had to wait for David to get back from mustering out. As I looked out of the window, I could see the large expanse of a huge bridge on one side and very tall buildings on the other side. I looked down below, into a very small courtyard, and saw a tiny tree in the square yard of the old building that was used to house arrivals from oversees. Looking out of the window, all by myself, I had some very serious doubts concerning my sanity, what had I done? "A tree grows in Brooklyn"...

But with great relief I heard David return. With him came his parents and sister, Mildred. They had rushed from Ohio to New York the minute they found out that we had landed. David had an older brother, Graham, a younger brother, Stenson, and the youngest, Mildred. I was welcomed properly into the family, all my fears were brushed away, and I was glad I had come; they were the parents to me that I had left behind in Europe. To this very day a deep love exists between us. Thank you God for answering every prayer.

I remember being in awe at the freedom that could be experienced in the United States. When my new father-in-law took us on a tour through New York in his car, he happened to get into the wrong lane on one of the wide boulevards.

> *The policeman stopped Dad, to find out where he wanted to go, and then to my amazement he did not get mad, but stopped traffic in the other lanes. Dad noticed the look of horror on my face, and later took me aside to explain to me, that there was nothing to fear from a policeman. This truly was a free country! What a wonder it all was!*

I was given a wonderful tour of the whole city of New York. I will never forget all the places I was taken to. There was the Empire State Building and Grant's Tomb, Chinatown and German Town and the Italian Section with all the wonderful little restaurants; there was Fifth Ave with the elegant shop windows and wonderful Times Square. I can still taste the piña colada that was served at the sidewalk stand. I had never had anything like it in my entire life. Oh, and the great American ice cream! I did not think I would ever get enough of it.

The morning we left New York was beautiful and bright and it was a joy to drive along the Hudson River, seeing things I had only heard of. Slowly we moved into the countryside and made our way to the capital of New York State. I remember it was hot in the afternoon, and there was a stillness in the air that made me almost listen to the things I saw with my eyes. The countryside grew larger and wider and in the distance we saw the Catskill Mountains. Our destination was coming into view, and soon we arrived at a very lovely old home. It was the home of David's uncle and aunt and their four girls.

Dad's brother was a pediatrician. Aunt Hedy was warm and full of laughter and one immediately felt at ease with her. I felt glad that I had come, because there was such warmth and a gracious feeling of welcome that made me no longer a stranger.

From there we made our way to Cleveland, Ohio, and it was in one of its lovely suburbs that David was at home. The rest of the trip went like a dream and I remember thinking how strange it was to really be here in this great big land, a stranger and yet not alone. There were many like me who had come seeking a new beginning, and I wondered how some of the ones that had come many years before me had felt. Had they been afraid? Had they been able to make their way? In the coming years I would meet many of them, from all the different places on earth that had come to this generous land that had a promise to all who worked hard, lived upright, and loved freedom.

David's hometown was small, some 15,000 inhabitants. The family was known by everybody because Dad had been in school work for many years.

We settled in. David and I each found a job. He worked for a local business and I found a job as a maintenance buyer for an industrial manufacturing company.

After several weeks we found a house to rent on the shore of Lake Erie, and I was introduced to some of my husband's friends. The home we rented was a furnished cottage right on the lake.

It was one of the most beautiful autumns. I can remember all the beauty of color as is the case in the Midwest. As the days grew shorter and shorter, the winds began to blow harder with every week. Finally the Christmas season approached and with it the wonder of all the memories past.

In the home we rented from a woman who spent her winters in the South, there was a room that was two stories high. It had a fireplace six feet wide made out of huge Lake Erie stones. It spread warmth into the large room on a blustery winter night. At night we heard the cracking and crunching of the ice on the lake, which was now solid enough to be walked out on for over a mile. Our large Christmas tree, some ten feet tall, was hung with gilded nuts and fresh apples, sweets, and cookies strung on strings. There were real candles on the tree, much to the horror of my mother-in-law. This, by the way, was the only time we did that! This was not the place where the tree was so fresh that it was still damp when one put it up and lit the candles on it.

The winter was long and cold that year, and I kept remembering the ones overseas. Some were long and dark. But this one was bright, with a certain view into the future. Because in the spring of the year, when the ice melted and the lake finally gave in to the warmth of the sun rays, we began to seriously look for a home of our own.

We bought a house, very small, but ours. It was but a block from the lake that we had come to love. It had a wonderful garden with lots of room to play in and to have a nice vegetable garden in. There were many flowering shrubs with a fragrance we enjoyed. We loved to bring some of the blossoms into the house. David brought home a cute little puppy, but we longed for children.

In May of 1962 I became a proud citizen of the United States of America. The experience was a stirring one. All the candidates for citizenship were led into one huge room of the courthouse in Cleveland. All of us had, more or less fervently, studied the history of the United States, and this was the day that we would be tested and could shine. We all came from countries where authorities were to be feared, and we just were not too sure of all of this.

In all different languages people helped each other to make ready for the test. I was sworn in that day. A brand new citizen. I was now part of a country that had a future, a hope. Now I could dare to visit my parents whom I had not seen for a long time.

Is my fear really gone? Did the black vulture finally get killed? Am I finally rid of the ugly remembrances of the past? Lord, if it still exists somewhere show me your strength to overcome!

It was a glorious visit. I remember, getting off the train in the nearby market town of Wels, Austria, and then waiting to get on the bus that would take me "home," as it had done so many times before. My anticipation rose. I could hardly wait to get to my destination. I started what seemed to be a long walk up the hill to the place that had been my home at one time. It seemed that it had been ages ago.

Much had happened in the years I had been away, but here the time stood still. There was still the mooing of the cows and the cackling of the hens; the wind still blew through the tops of the pine trees and made that forlorn sound I so loved. There was that wonderful smell again of food lovingly cooked for a family, for it was close to five o'clock in the afternoon. I almost expected someone in the family to stick his head out the window and call me in for dinner. Mama and Papa and my brother Helmut knew I was coming home sometime that day. I could just see my mom in her usual kitchen apron, with reddened cheeks and a string of hair falling into her eyes, cooking up a storm. And so it was. Oh, what joy filled all of our hearts to see each other again after almost five years. All the goodies I liked Mama cooked for me. I felt like the son come home to the feast of the fatted calf.

This was a wonderful visit. I was forever grateful that I did go that summer because my beloved Papa died that following New Year's Eve. A complication after surgery for cancer, they said. I grieved because I could not go to be with the rest of the family in Austria. My poor Papa would not have to suffer any more.

Instead of going over to Europe for Papa's funeral, we felt it would be good for Mama to come and visit us and spend some time with us. My cousin Hansi, whom I had not seen for several years, wanted to come with her two children and accompany Mama on her trip to the United States. Little did we know, when we agreed with these plans, that our own family would have a considerable increase in number.

Oh, how I would miss him! It was as if a voice deep within me said: trust me; let go, my child; you are not alone. It was the price to pay for following my heart. It is the same price one pays when following the Lord.

Boston, 1997

What am I going to do? I am pregnant! And he cares nothing about it! Where will I go with a baby? My parents don't want me at their home. Is it right to get an abortion? That's what he wants and my parents too. But oh, God, this is my baby! I cannot just go and have it killed! I know I have totally messed up my life with this pregnancy. It will never be the same again for me no matter what I decide. I don't have many options. Get an abortion; keep the baby; give it up for adoption. One is murder and I don't know if I can live with the memory of it. The second one is a dead end street for me and a life for my child that lacks all the promise one desires for children. The third is the most selfless of the options, and I know that the sorrow of it all will almost overtake me! Oh, God forgive me. Somehow I must make the decision. I will give up my little one to someone who yearns for a child. God, will they love this baby like I could? Please look out for this little bundle all through its life....

CHAPTER 19

A Full Family

WE HAD FOR SEVERAL YEARS longed to have children. We had been to doctors; we had treatments to help conception to no avail. Finally, on the urging of my physician, we applied to several agencies to become adoptive parents. We agreed to take in two children, siblings, because we really did not want to have just one child.

David had taken a new job that took us away from our beloved Lake Erie, and we relocated in the country in southern Ohio. That was God's plan. Again we were at a place at a time that was right and ordained to be. The home we had found was in the rolling hills of the countryside. It was next to a murmuring brook that cooled the yard ever so nicely in the hot summer sun. There were horses right behind us, and sometimes the farmer let us ride them. It was in this setting that the Lord allowed us to become truly a family.

When I first heard of them, my heart jumped and I called my husband, who during that particular week was traveling in Indiana. They had called me. There are two boys. From one family. Could he be home quickly? We needed to talk about the possibility of having some visitors with us over the weekend. Perhaps they would come to stay? And so he hurried home.

I remember it well. It was on July 20. A stifling hot day. A Saturday. Early that morning we prepared two bedrooms for two boys that we were to pick up and host for a weekend to see if this really was what we wanted.

We arrived at the agency and were ushered into one of the rooms, and then they brought three children in. Not two. (Two brothers and a sister, all of the same family.) The girl, Carolyn, was five years old, with beautiful blond hair and the most questioning blue eyes, which seemed to inquire what was going to happen to them now. Were they going to be shoved from one home to the other? Or was this a place that they would call home someday? Who were these two people who had come to look at them? What are you going to do with my boys? Carolyn was most possessive of her two younger brothers. She was the one who had dressed Paul and seen to it that he ate his food. No doubt she kept the two of them in line. She was slender, had long legs and a light complexion, and looked very German. She had become old beyond her years.

Dale, three-and-a-half years old, was tall like his sister, but his complexion was a beautiful olive one, with brown eyes and dark hair that had been cut quite short. He was shy in comparison to his sister and brother. But he had a quick laugh and he longed for a hug, even though it was hard for him to submit to it. He was still hurting because of the absence of his real father and grandmother.

Paul, one-and-a-half years old, was blond and brown-eyed. Strong-willed, the youngest of the three and very much attached to Carolyn. He was a compulsive eater and had to be curbed in his eating habit. At our first meal, which of course was the All-American hot dog, Paul at eighteen months ate three hot dogs plus, plus. He had short little legs and a short, strong neck that made me wonder how he would look when he got old. He turned into a handsome young man.

Right then and there it became clear that one could not separate three siblings this close in age. After a short conference with the nurse on duty, we decided to take home not two, but three children.

It became obvious after two hours that all three children had something besides a cold. In fact, when we called the doctor, who came to the house, he diagnosed all three of them as having whooping cough. The youngest one was in serious trouble since he was under two years old. My schedule, which was directed by an alarm clock day and night, called for the administering of medicine at three different times and in different strengths. Add to that the absence of clothing! One had to wash and iron one or two times a day until we got new clothing for all three. We gratefully received the gift of two pairs of shoes for all three children. Did someone say they are cheaper by the dozen? I can tell you that from none to three isn't bad either! I immediately quit my job and became a full-time mother.

> *Lord, is this why I have not been able to have children of my own? Because there were these three little ones needing a home? How amazing your ways are! What are you preparing me for?*

The adventures of the early life of the kids would take another book to fill, but suffice it to say that we were thrilled with our little bundles and were eagerly becoming parents.

I learned to apply all the things I had learned at the good old convent school. Cook and bake and can fruits for the next year; sew clothing for all the children and myself; keep a garden for fresh food; take care of a dog; entertain business people and friends. On and on it went. Ten days after the children came to live with us we moved our family to southern Ohio. Several days after our move, my mother and my cousin with her two children came to visit with us.

I was so glad to see Mama but it was a hard adjustment for the whole family, because not only did the children have to adjust to us and a new environment, there were also two other children and a new grandmother, which was especially hard for Dale because he had loved his own grandmother who was no longer here!

It was like a big merry-go-round at times. First there were none, and then there were three of our own and two cousins! From two people to nine people. It was not easy, but we managed. The children considered us their parents right away. I often thought it might have been the fact that we "kept" them even through the whooping cough. I became reconciled to the fact that I was not raising someone else's children, but that I had three of my own. All I had to go by was the way I was raised, with discipline and order, and so I set out with this my new family to do the same. At times I thought perhaps I was a bit too strict, but then I remembered my own home. A few years later I was glad. All the order and discipline allowed us to relax a bit after the children got older.

Our family grew. We had all the ups and downs that families experience when raising children. But they always were a joy to me and a gift of God.

In the fall of 1967, it became apparent that Carolyn, who now was nine years old, had become subject to terrible allergies that plagued her day and night. Her asthma attacks became very strong, and we as a family did all we could to help her. It was through the sickness of this child that the Lord would again bring me into a closer relationship with Himself.

When all failed to help Carolyn in Ohio, we took a trip to Florida. We thought that perhaps a change of environment might prove to be helpful. We found that she responded to the warm weather much better than her mother did. So we decided to move. Dave's employer allowed him to open up a new territory in the South. He was able to stay with the same company. Spanish Fort, Alabama, was our final destination. I remember arriving there one very warm October night.

My mother had come from Austria. This was the second time she had crossed the ocean. Traveling south from Ohio, she had a hard time imagining any place as big as the states we had just traveled through. But as daylight came, she approved of David's choice of a home for us.

Almost immediately after we settled in, Mama became very ill, and within two days she was dead. No one had ever known she was so ill, and I was grateful to the Lord she did not have to suffer long. Blocked intestines. Possibly cancer. Deadly. But it was not easy on us. Again, it was the Lord that helped me through a rough time. He sent me prayer warriors and helpers to minister to me and the family. This was especially needed since within two weeks Carolyn landed in the hospital having had a very bad attack. I can still see her pleading for me to stay, and yet I could not. I had two other children at home and a husband who was out of town. I left her in good hands and reassured her that I would be back first thing in the morning. That night she sneaked her way to the nurses' station and tried to call me at home. When the nurse called me to talk to Carolyn, I wept.

There was no way I could have gone through all of this without the strong arm of Jesus. This time I knew it.

We became aware of the fact that Carolyn's attacks would come and go. I learned to give adrenaline shots if needed. It was also necessary to do some detective work, observing reactions to different foods, etc. During this time, God spoke to me very clearly through Carolyn, the little girl who had learned to love the Lord through prayers and the support of church friends. In her own way she was a witness to many people of the goodness of the Lord.

As I drew to the Lord for strength, I realized that there was more than I had ever dreamed could be. I tried to ask "spiritual" people about it but they were not of any help to me. It seemed they did not understand what it was, I was looking for.

There it was again, that longing, that beckoning of the Spirit of God that I did not quite understand but could see the signs of all around me. It was as if the Lord was getting me ready for something. For maybe a trial or tribulation, a blessing? What is it God? Prepare me.

What was this gnawing deep inside me, that would not let me come to rest. It awakened me in the middle of the night, not in fright but in wonder. I became quite used to it. At times I looked forward to being awake, so I could pray and think and read the Bible and learn. For many months I did this, night after night, but strangely enough I was never weary in the daytime, never tired. I was like a soldier made ready for war.

And then the battle began. In the early spring of 1971 we knew that Dave's business would be one of the many that crumbled under the economic crisis that had effected industry. I am sure he was devastated. Being the breadwinner in the family, it must have been a large burden for him to carry.

We lost the business, but we did not go into bankruptcy. We promised to pay back all debt within the next ten years. Gratefully we were able to accomplish it.

Our home was almost sold out from under us. A Christian friend, who thought it worth investing in our lives, bought our home. He let us rent it until such a time as we could buy it back from him. Again, by the grace of God, we were able to do that.

If anyone had asked me how I felt at that moment, I would have said: strengthened. Strengthened? what a strange thing to say in a situation like it. But it was true: I knew that the God who had become more real to me in the past months gave me strength to carry on.

I was forty years old and my body bounced back and came to meet the need of the hour. The boys needed me. Carolyn was back in school. She excelled in school that year, and we had high hopes for her future.

Being alone with the children because of David's extensive traveling, I became a very light sleeper. I heard everything. The slightest shift of their bodies made me aware of them. There were many nights when I was up and taking care of our frightened little girl, struggling for breath. Again it was Jesus who strengthened me, not to panic but to quietly minister to Carolyn.

That was in April 1971.

Three months later, July 20, 1971, exactly eight years after our adopting her, out of the blue, feeling better than she had in a long time, Carolyn went home to be with her heavenly Father. A blood clot, they said.

Charlotte, a neighbor, came to watch the two boys while we rushed to the hospital.

I remember saying to the Lord following the ambulance on the way to the hospital: Please don't let her die Lord, but if it is to be, I trust you.

Later I thought: What a strange thing I had said! But I know that God honored this expression of trust toward Him. He showed Himself strong where I was weak, and He kept me steadfast to nurture the other two children.

The doctors labored to revive her, but it was not the will of our heavenly Father. She had gone home. Our sweet little girl, so full of the joy of the Lord and full of nonsense at times, was no more with us. We could not touch her anymore, her little poems and pictures could not be found on my dresser anymore, after she had gone to bed at night. The boys were in shock. One of her brothers would not let anybody go into her room, he hurt so badly. The other brother remembered the spats they had had and, childishly having wished her dead at times, he repented of being very human.

Her friends grieved and were frightened because it brought their own mortality into focus. They remembered that, just the week before, this blond laughing girl had been on a Girl Scout campout and enjoyed the company of all the giggling teenagers.

We did allow her to live life to the fullest. She was the one who set the limits of her activities. Who decided that she would like to go with the rest of her friends to Girl Scout camp even though she knew it would make her very sick. "I came that you might have life and have it more abundantly." I remember letting go and praying for God to bring her back home again to us. Oh, how He built faith into me that year!

There was no funeral, only a memorial service to remember Carolyn Yvonne Patterson, thirteen years old and loved by all who knew her. The Spanish Fort Presbyterian Church was filled with people. The ones that could not find room stood in the courtyard beyond the large double doors at the back of the church. All of her schoolmates were there and all her Girl Scout friends. The neighbors and members of our congregation, and many people of other churches in the small town, crowded into the service.

The young people of the congregation came to be with us almost round the clock. They came to bring us their sacrifice of love. I remember wearing a white suit to underscore the celebration of complete healing for our Carolyn. For she was healed and safe for eternity with Jesus.

There was a steady stream of friends coming to our door to bring strength. Many of them left having been strengthened. God's love flowed among all of us and we had joy even in sadness.

God, in His mercy, let us find a letter she wanted to send to a young singer she admired. In it she explained that nothing was worth the peace of knowing that one is a child of the King: not fame, not fortune, not friends. She went on to say that she knew this without a doubt because, in her sickness, the Lord had shown himself strong. "One could see it all around one," she said, "in the love of family, friends, and in the peace that passes all understanding even in frightful situations."

There were times when I could hear her calling me, or so I thought, in broad daylight, because I had been so used to her voice calling me. But she was with her heavenly father whom she loved. What a blessing it is to know without a shadow of a doubt that some day we will again see her because she, like her family, is His child.

Sadly, my husband could not be reached by me, or anyone else. It was so hard to watch him in his agony, and yet there was nothing I could do but pray and love him. He became withdrawn and finally at times very depressed. This is when God began to move in his life. How would he respond?

New Orleans, Louisiana, 1998
Let's see, how many years have we been married? 24 years? A long time. Enough time to know all the strength and weakness of my husband. I do still love him but it is not easy to live with him. I feel like I am in boat that rocks terribly in an ongoing storm. I do so yearn for peace in our household. I wish I knew what I can do to help this situation. I want to save my marriage…

CHAPTER 20

The Renewal

THE NEXT FEW YEARS WENT BY and our family grew up. There were the typical joys and sorrows of a growing family. The victories and the defeats. The good grades, the lost ball games, the broken relationships and those that blossomed. Some new dreams to dream and some older ones to put away. But all through it I felt the strong hand of the Lord God holding us up in a very special way. I knew that there was more and I went forth to pursue it—whatever it was!

My only sadness was that my husband suffered more and more emotionally as time went on. I could tell as I watched him, and I was helpless. There was no one to tell about it except God. God is a patient listener, a true Prince of Peace. As I clung closer to the Lord than ever, the yearning I had as a young girl was present in my life again. What was it? Could it be true that one could have not only the assurance of eternal life but also the blessing of His presence daily as one went about one's business?

I threw myself into work with the church and in the community I lived in, which was not anything new for me. There had been honors in the past: Citizen of the Year, Woman of the Year, President of the Women of the Church. There no doubt would have been more of them, but they became increasingly uninteresting and unimportant. There had to be more.

I examined my life. Yes, I had things in the proper perspective: I loved God and enjoyed being in church with my friends to worship; I loved my husband and my family; I was a good wife, loyal, fair, and faithful; I watched over and disciplined my children in the absence of my traveling husband; I went to all their ball games, all their concerts, all the important Scout gatherings, piano ensembles, etc. I lived in a very nice home, spacious and nicely furnished, I drove a relatively new car, and I never thought myself to be poor. I knew without a shadow of a doubt that I was saved. So then why was I so restless, searching, pondering and yearning?

And then one evening a friend asked me to come to a special prayer meeting of some "European Catholics," and I went, not because I wanted to go, but simply to get rid of the friend, who I knew to be a bit, shall we say, "fanatic." I was a bit embarrassed and yet it was all very interesting but... How in the world could I go along with what I heard people say there about healing and the Holy Spirit. There was no way that my husband... "Oh, ye of little faith," the Spirit whispered into my ear.

At any rate, I decided that this was the last time that I would go to any such meeting, and I told my friend so. But the wind of the Spirit blows, and where it lands only He knows. All week I could not get rid of the thoughts of hearing songs that were strange to me and yet so familiar that I could after one chorus enter into singing them. How? Finally it was time for another prayer meeting on a Thursday evening. A force that I had never before encountered with such urgency made me forget what I had said to my friend, and I called her and asked to come along, just that one night, if you please.

It was another July 20. The year was 1978. Halfway through the teaching of the evening, the teachers felt that someone wanted to be baptized in the Holy Spirit. As if watching myself from across the way, I noticed that it was I who raised my hand. Through the one ministering, the Spirit said that He had waited for me for a long time. And I knew He was right. I did not feel anything. I did not see anything, there was no swaying or speaking on my part, but I knew what I had received, because I had found it in the Bible: the promise.

What I found in the Bible I believed and what I believed, I received. No one, being human or supernatural, could ever make me believe otherwise.

It was at this juncture in my life that I decided I could not afford to wait for my husband to come along with me on my spiritual journey. Somehow there was an urgency that I felt to go on. To learn, to ponder things deep in my heart. I had no idea at this point in my life how I would have to depend on all the things that I was learning in the next few years. But God did.

The Holy Spirit kept stirring me. It was truly supernatural the amount of knowledge I took in, both in my head and in my heart. I used every available free minute to learn. My husband was not too pleased about it, but he did come along for a while and learned. Then he decided he preferred tennis with a friend in his leisure time to the things of the Lord. Grieving, I stepped back to let him pursue his own interests.

But the Lord is kind and generous: He gave me a friend unlike any friend I had ever had before: June. She and I rejoiced together in the Lord. We learned and taught each other. Rarely does one have the opportunity to be that transparent with another human being, with a friend. She and I encouraged each other and corrected each other. Soon we saw the results of it. There was not only a bond but an understanding of when to speak and when not. There was a strength that was being put into us supernaturally, that we truly could not understand nor see until much later. And our guideline was the Holy Scripture. How we loved to read and pore over the Bible and the Word that says that we should read it and think on it when we are sitting down or resting in bed, when we are walking, talking, singing, or thinking came true; it not only gave us strength, it renewed our mind. This process was not a short one, but one we had "purposed in our heart" to follow. And the Lord blessed this determination to follow Him by making us more steadfast than we ever thought we could be.

For both June and I walked on this new avenue that the Lord had opened for us, steadfastly putting one foot in front of the other. To say that this was a solemn time for us is only partially true. Many of our friends can still remember the gales of laughter whenever they saw us at the store or at any other place. In fact we both remember a time when one of our neighbors, seeing us at the store, commented that he always worried when he saw us together anywhere. No one ever knew what might happen and most of the time it was hilarious. Oh, Lord, how you knew I would need this encouragement in but a short time.

My preparation for God's plan had begun.

Kosovo, March 1999

All around me I saw life. New life coming into the world in a refugee tent. How the mother must have felt when she first knew her time had come! No home, her husband was not with her. Was he alive somewhere? Or had he been one of those who were shot? Where would they all live? Oh, God, whom can I trust with my other children!... We Kosovo women remember that there was another time like it in this century. I remember my mother telling about it. She was ready to give birth to a little baby. She was alone. Oh, where was Papa? In Russia or in Poland? Unlike me, she had four walls around her—but for how long? The bombs were falling all around, and she could not get to the doctor's office; there was no way she could make her way to the hospital. No cars, no streetcars, no buses, no ambulance. Oh, God, let this little one be healthy so there will not be any complications!

CHAPTER 21

The Next Generation

THERE IS A TIME AND A SEASON FOR EVERYTHING in this life. This was the start of a new season.

I knew that my son Paul and his wife Kathy were expecting a baby. I prayed for them and the unborn child. The Lord directed me in a very particular prayer. He showed me that I had an older brother who was born and died very shortly after his birth. And that before that there was a similar death in my grandparents' offspring. Then there was the death of our own Carolyn who was also the oldest child in the family. This baby was to be the firstborn in my son's family. I was to surround this child with prayers similar to a protective wall around a city. And so I did.

In the beginning of September 1984, during the wild winds of a hurricane, my precious first grandchild was born. He came two weeks early because of a complication. How blessed we were that there were doctors and ambulances and a hospital to go to, and that my son was at home with his wife to comfort her and to do what needed to be done. Thank you, Lord, for showing me the importance of prayer.

The baby was called Joseph Paul. A boy! He was healthy and beautiful! What joy must have filled their hearts. Oh Lord, I pondered, that name, what an example to follow. Make him honorable and strong and full of zeal for the things of the Lord, like his namesakes, I prayed.

I went to North Carolina to be with the children and to help with the new arrival. It was wonderful to watch the tiny fingers grasping at the things held out for him, the little feet moving restlessly as if they had many places to go. It was so amazing to see my own children in this little boy. There was much happiness in the small apartment Paul and Kathy lived in, and the days flew by much too quickly. Too soon it was time to go back home again. My heart was full of joy. I was bubbling over.

I remember receiving a call from David while I was in North Carolina, inquiring about the baby, and when I told him about the joy and happiness in the home where this little newborn bundle was, I broke down and wept. "We can make the same kind of start again, David," I said. A strange quiet hung over the phone. But I had made up my mind that I would once more intensify my efforts to bring about a healing to a relationship that lacked life.

As I enjoyed being with the newborn baby, I sensed that something was wrong but dismissed it. After being with them for two weeks, I came back home and eagerly awaited the return of my husband on Friday night, to tell him all the good news of our family.

Soon I knew what my unrest had been. After the usual greeting with a hug and kiss in the driveway David entered our home. I felt a shadow move in with him, and soon I knew what it was. I had sensed it over the past few weeks. He declared that he wanted a divorce immediately. I was devastated and tried to talk to him about it. But he seemed very angry and was not interested in any conversation.

It was very difficult for me to realize that this man with whom I had shared twenty-eight years of my life suddenly no longer wanted anything to do with me. I did not want a divorce, and my first impulse was: If I don't want a divorce, then I cannot be forced to be divorced! Wrong! It does not work that way. In my heart I knew it was so. My husband did not even want to stay in our home any more that night, and he left.

I got in the car and drove around trying to clear my head, hoping I would wake up out of this nightmare in a while and it would all be over. Our relationship had at times become difficult, and I had carried my burden to the Lord. I began to do the same now. And yet I yearned to have a friend put her arms around me and let me talk, or help me decide, or let me cry, or do whatever it was I should be doing right then. I was confused. Some of our mutual friends were confused. Some were in shock. Some were angry. Some prayed with me and loved me during this difficult time. It was as if unselfish tithing of time and emotions with others in the past had just been blessed a hundredfold.

I hurt so bad that I thought holding onto my chest would stop the pain in the middle of my body. I had only known one other pain like it: the pain I had when another relationship died: Carolyn.

Oh, Lord, how, why...what will I do? My whole life fell apart, it simply was not fair....What would it do to the Christian witness in my life?

During a time of prayer June encouraged me. She said that the Lord would get Glory out of this situation. Even though I believed it, I wondered how in the world this could happen? Oh, how I underestimated God!

He spoke to me through a member of the congregation: "Do not defend yourself, the Body will be your defense." "Guard your emotions, for Jesus will be your friend and your husband and your counselor." And He was and is all that and much, much more.

Oh, God, that is why there had been such an urgency to draw close unto you! You know the past; you are in the present; and you see the future. Thank you for preparing and directing me.

During this time, when I was busy with work and getting on with life, I had very few extra moments. God sent me people who, like me, were hurting but not finding a solution to their problem. They saw something in me. Call it a light of hope, a sign of God's strength. A steady endurance. Call it whatever you will, it gave me a chance to share how the Lord had helped me to cope during a very difficult time.

I knew that my children would have a very hard time dealing with this. Many of our friends would have to take this to the Lord over and over again, as this painful experience drifted in and out of their lives.

After many heartaches, injustices, unbelievable exhibitions of cruelty, brashness beyond belief, I no longer recognized the man I had loved and married twenty-eight years earlier, and finally in May of 1985 the divorce decree became final. It was over.

The change in the man I loved made it a little easier for me to cope and agree to the divorce. It was the Lord who showed me that even He did not force anyone to love him. I could not expect to be able to do that with my husband. I do know however, that the scars of rejection are deep, and the wholeness can only come if one is willing to let the Lord do the healing.

I was alone. My husband remarried within three months. I would from then on daily speak out forgiveness toward him, even though I knew, that the unforgiveness in my own heart was not shed. For two-and-a-half years I made myself available to the Lord to work this emotional freedom into my life. He is a faithful Father. He did. Totally. One day when I began my prayer the heart-wrenching emotion was gone. What a God we have!

The divorce left me in a rather unfortunate condition. I had almost no money, and, because my husband did not want me to work, I had never really received any particular training to be competitive in the marketplace. The decree provided me with the car, which had been paid for but was by now six years old, with the large house we had shared for twenty years. It had two mortgages on it. There was no alimony for me, since there were no children under the age of twenty-one.

I believe that it took a while for me to come to the conclusion that in my own strength I had only a small chance of ever being able to maintain my residence. Somehow this was very important to me at this moment of my life, and it was not until later that I gladly exchanged this temporary security for the provision of the Lord.

Since I was left with debts, and I knew that the Lord does not look kindly upon people who do not fulfill their commitment, I had to work two and three jobs. I immediately found a job at a local department store, which proved to be a very nice experience. It provided for me the basic mortgage payment plus some of the utilities. It gave me group insurance in case I needed it. The second job I had was freelance interior decorating, hanging wallpaper personally for each customer I worked with. The third regular job was that of typing sales reports for a salesman friend of the family, which provided me with my gasoline money for the month. Besides that, I catered a wedding now and then and made articles for some of the local craft shows. A woman friend's daughter who went to college in Mobile needed a sheltered place to live, and I rented one of our bedrooms and bathrooms to her with the privileges of the kitchen and living room.

It was a busy time. My schedule was so complicated some weeks that I should have had a secretary to keep me straight. Many times I had no days off during the whole week, save perhaps a free morning or some afternoon. But the Lord used it like good medicine and saw to it that all my needs were met.

There was no time to even think of having a pity party! All the times I had fed my spirit were now a treasure. For out of me poured for myself and all who heard me or came in contact with me life, abundant life. That which was very hard at times for the family to do—to meet our commitments—was met by me with poorly paying jobs and God's provision. He became truly Jehovah my provider.

The Lord not only provided for my natural needs, He gave me a church family who truly cared and were my defense. I worked, had fellowship with family and friends, and most of the time was not aware of anything unusual. I drew close to the Lord and somehow there must have been something about me that people became aware of. Where at one point I had wondered about my Christian witness, I no longer needed to wonder. It was intact. Again my prayers had been answered.

> *There was this strong stirring in the center of my being to do, I knew not what! But I knew it was God. I could and wanted to follow whatever it was that the Lord had for me. I had no encumbrance. I was free to be obedient even if I did not understand it all.*

I am scared. I have no problem teaching small intimate groups. I have done that for many years. But to take over a program. Please God, I have absolutely no training for this sort of thing! But they need somebody! Why should it be me? I know; it is time to give back some of the blessings I have received. It is time to put my money where my mouth is! I say God can do anything. Please God, prove it!

CHAPTER 22

The Call

It was about that time that my church asked me to work with young marrieds and singles. Even though I obviously had not done everything right in my marriage, I knew what it was that had been wrong. All the years my marriage was one of little real in-depth communication. There was less and less to be said until one day there was none.

And whereas I longed to rebuild the relationship, because it had been good at one time, it cannot be done unless both parties want to put the effort into it and, with the guidance of the Word of God, rebuild something that seems totally broken. It must be said here however, for anyone who has the same problem I had in my marriage, that if both parties are Christian, it must be attempted. And it can be done.

The class was a blessing to me and every one of the class members is as dear to me now as they were then. I believe God used all that He had put into me in the past few years and it was good training.

In October of 1987 I more and more became aware of the fact that my security was totally in the Lord ,and that somewhere, somehow, God would use my natural ability of the German language, but I just didn't understand how that could all work together. God was again moving in my life and I was eager to follow.

Would I become one of those people who packed up their belongings and went wherever the Lord sent them? Me? I had no training! Or did I? What is it that the Lord considers training?

I remembered being at a Day of Encouragement for Women back in 1978, and even though this was the first time I had been in this particular church, the guest speaker, during the second part of the meeting, spoke to me prophetically. I had never even heard of such a thing, let alone known anyone who had received prophecy. She said, among other things, that the Lord God would make a way for me to walk in, that from now on mountains would literally be overcome, and the Lord my God would stand to my side and be my strength; I would sing a new song that I had never sung before.

My pastors had individually at one time or another spoken the same kind of things to me, and, being the kind of person I am, I did not immediately act on it but pondered all these things. The strange pulling in my inner being. What was happening to me?

God did speak to people very clearly when they listened. I knew I had been set free, there were no more encumbrances if I would only step out in faith. I was free to follow God. This too was preparation.

In November 1987, my son and his family, who were at this time living in Germany, asked me to consider living with them for a year, or however long I wanted to.

They were expecting a baby in May of 1988, and Joey longed for his Oma, as I longed for all of them. The children not only had a need, they felt I had worked far too many hours for what? To maintain a house that no longer was a home except to me. They were right, I thought, and again I pondered... How, Lord? What, Lord?

Within less than a month, a friend of my church, and an always welcome guest, spoke to me. This time I recognized the Word of the Lord. I would be in ministry at the place where my roots were. She then spoke to me about her work in Europe with a missionary organization. She asked me to pray about the possibility of traveling with her behind the Iron Curtain in a women's teaching ministry. I did pray; but how Lord? How? All this stuff I have!

This was before Christmas. and my family would be visiting at Christmas time.

It seemed that there was a time coming to make decisions. How would I fare? But I knew my Lord! He never asked anything of me that was impossible! What, Lord? How?

As I turned all this over and over in my head, it came to me: In Scripture as the Lord's call came to the servant, the servant had to get ready. How could I go to be with my children, or to travel on the Lord's behalf, if I had things that hung around my neck like an albatross. And so I began.

Tirana, Albania, 1998

I thought I brought with me what we needed. We didn't really think it would take such a long time to get back home again. And now, in this camp, I am not so sure. I am not sure of anything! Why did I not bring more bedding for the family? Or some of the jam I had down in the basement? We were in such a hurry to get out. Now, as I think about it, I wonder if we will ever see the old town again. Poor Agron! I wonder what they did with my brother! Oh, God protect him. He is so young!

CHAPTER 23

Freedom

How does one start to dismantle one's home? Well, no problem, one starts by cleaning out closets. I want to tell you right here that if you ever are called to do a particular thing, for the Lord or not, that is not a bad idea and an overwhelming task.

Have you looked into your closets lately? Do you know what all has been stored away for years and years? It seems there were the children's first booties and their last baseball uniform; the Girl Scout insignia and the old games that had been tattered when they were last used. If anyone ever loved to do puzzles, it must have been our family. There were enough puzzles to fill an entire store. And games! The local senior citizens meeting room would have been proud to have that many!

Then there were all the patterns that I had, at one time or other, sewn. All the stacks of fabric that had not been sewn yet. Some of them had been out of style for many years! There were all the odds and ends I had used to make all the little and big gift items sold at the craft shows. There were sheets for beds, magazines with interesting ideas for a possible Christmas gift. It seems there were thousands of issues of *National Geographic;* books with house plans—in case I would build another house!

Not to speak of all the records and the cassette tapes, of the books and the various files filled with bits and pieces of interesting information for this and that occasion. Or the three-ring binders I had personally filled with more information than many classrooms had to offer.

The list goes on and on. And I had barely begun!

I had not even dared to start in the kitchen. What will one keep and what get rid of? Right then and there I decided that some of my friends had, at one time or other, admired this or that in our home. So I knew who would get the picture of the laughing Christ, the shadowbox for miniatures, baskets and boxes; this and that. In the middle of many an hour of sifting my life for important and unimportant things, there came the question over and over: Am I doing the right thing? Is this what you want, Lord? I had heard of all the various people who had, out of their own emotions, taken a step like this only to become shipwrecked at some point later.

I am not sure how people heard that I was moving! But by the first week in February I was asked if I would care to sell my dining room furniture. I sure did! From then on it was like a huge avalanche. Requests for furniture to be bought from me, electric appliances, tools, utensils, and on it went. All the while I went to work to at least two jobs and in my spare time I made ready to go.

Before all the selling of furniture started I painfully became aware of a problem. I desperately needed to have dental work done. I had gum disease and it had to be taken care of if I ever wanted to go anywhere on anyone's behalf.

The problem was the expense of it. I had hardly spoken a word to anyone about this when I received word, through my pastor, that someone wished to prepare me in this area by taking on the cost of my dental work over and above my insurance. I could hardly believe it! Why, Lord? Why for me?

In spite of all the tales of horror about gum surgery I had a minimum of pain. In fact, after the second surgery I met with friends at an Italian restaurant and ate with them. Soft stuff, but I ate.

One day on my way to the dentist I was overwhelmed with all of the "things" that had to be done. My weary disposition gave in to a giant pity party. I complained to the Lord that I had no one to help me with the task at hand; that there was no husband who could help me with all the red tape and the physical work. Poor me...

Through the tears, which made me stop the car, the Lord spoke to my heart. He gave me a Scripture to look up. This was not a usual experience for me! Isaiah 54, the voice inside me said. I knew what it said in Isaiah 53. But the only thing I recalled in

Isaiah 54 was: "no weapon formed against you shall prosper." At the first opportunity, much later that day, I looked up the verses in Isaiah 54. I wept as I recognized the total provision of Jesus, my Lord. The fifty-fourth chapter of Isaiah is the story of my life. It is the promise for my future. The Lord knew how badly I needed this for my direction. I had been encouraged by my God, who cares about everything I do. I was full of joy and anticipation.

As one reads that Scripture, it is sort of a replay of my adult life, and I knew that Jesus recognized my pain and wanted to pour soothing oil on it. That He wanted to encourage me, strengthen me, and tell me that He was pleased with me. It was so important to me to know, as I set out on this new path with him, that there would be no "weapon formed against me that would prosper." He showed me that this was my "heritage from Him" and that my "righteousness" came from Him.

God, you know how to get through to anyone. Even a hard headed person like me! This is my story! Yes, I will trust you! Have you read my story so far? Read the account in Isaiah 54 and you will recognize much of it!

This was my last pity party.

I thanked the Lord for all the small and large answers to prayers and needs. I continued to meet Him with every decision about the furniture, the car, till I found myself almost ready.

I had decided to put my children's furniture, which I had stored in my garage, and the items I saved for myself into a storage room. When I got back I would not need much. A bed, two chairs, a desk, some end tables, some rugs. For my children I saved the family silver, china, and glassware, plus antique items that were of interest to them.

I purchased an airline ticket for a flight to Frankfurt, Germany, one way...what a strange feeling! I was to leave on Pentecost Sunday, May 22, 1988. The excitement began to mount. I had burned my bridges behind me. There were still a lot of things that had to be taken care of. I really did not know how the Lord would do all of that.

By now I knew, I was out of control....God was in control.

Finally there was a garage full of boxes left, which had to be sorted through and sold or given away. Halfheartedly I put an ad in the local paper for a Friday morning 8:00 a.m. garage sale.

I thought that the Salvation Army would always be glad to take whatever I did not need or want. At 7:00 a.m. there was a driveway full of cars, and all up and down the street people waited to see what I had to sell. I was overwhelmed. That day I sold over a thousand dollars' worth of items that I did not think anyone would want. Someone came and asked if I wanted to sell my car to them; if I did, they would be glad to let me use it until the day before I left. Wow! God, you do have everything under control!

As the day came to a close, I was exhausted. While I was closing the doors of my garage, one more customer drove up. He and his wife had been there earlier. He wanted to know if there was anything in the work shed in the backyard that he might be able to use. I told him to please help himself to anything he could use. This he did and even paid me for it. He came back the next morning with his truck. Anything that was left after the Goodwill people had picked up what they wanted, he took and disposed of it for me. So even this detail was taken care of.

But now, Lord, comes the "biggie"! What are you going to do about the house? I had put a sign up in the front yard some days earlier: HOUSE FOR SALE BY OWNER and the telephone number where I could be reached. The sign was about two feet by three; it was yellow with black writing because someone had told me that those two colors would be easier to see than any other color. During the first night it was out on the lawn, it rained. The sign had almost totally wrapped itself around the pole it was fastened to. Nobody could have read the phone number. Except God.

My house was in a very nice residential area. But it was one of three homes for sale right next to each other. One family had moved ,and the other had a death in the family. One house had been on the market for three years, the other for one year. Fat chance for me to sell a house the way I went about it! But God in His infinite wisdom knew!

Friends had taken in some foster children and were in desperate need of a larger home. There was a slight problem.

They had a home to sell themselves. Until they did sell their home they did not have the money to buy another one. Nor did they have enough money to come up with the large amount of equity that my home demanded. It seemed impossible.

And yet, I felt right about doing what I was about to do. My friends and I sat down and put our cards on the table. Here we were, two Christian parties, both of whom should be able to rejoice with the outcome of this situation. They did not have the necessary cash to buy the home outright; I needed a certain amount of money to start out with and to have someone in the house who would faithfully pay both mortgages and the taxes and the insurance. Someone who could take care of any and all repairs while I was gone. They needed a larger home, preferably to buy at the end of one year.

We agreed. Almost with a handshake, but to appease families and friends we went to a lawyer to set this down on paper. He thought this very irregular but he finally went along with us and so it was that two days before my departure I signed my home away.

Well, Lord, I am free, I thought. What now?

I have complained and complained about how I was treated by my friends. People have listened but nothing has changed. In fact I feel worse than ever about it! Then somebody came to see me and asked me to forgive them because they had said things that had proved to be wrong. I simply had to forgive someone for stealing my good name. My speaking out forgiveness, I could see, made a difference to them. Maybe that was the way to begin my own restoration process? Oh, I don't know…and yet what do I have to lose? Okay. I do forgive them. There. What do you know! It makes me feel better!

CHAPTER 24

Coming Full Circle

ONE MORE THING HAPPENED. I want you to know, God is equally as interested in the practical everyday aspects of our lives as He is interested in the emotional and spiritual well being of His children.

He allowed me to make peace with two people from my past, one a young person asking my forgiveness and one a friend who was gravely ill. I knew that some forgiving and being forgiven had to be done, and I decided to go and visit. We spoke; I asked forgiveness for anger directed toward her because of a very painful situation, and she and I were reconciled. Several weeks later this person died. I thanked God for allowing me to make peace.

And finally one evening, friends and I went to take care of a very personal thing that meant a lot to both of my boys and myself. We took the urn that contained the ashes of my beautiful little Carolyn and with prayers and thanksgiving for her life we sprinkled the remains of her earthly body over the waters of Mobile Bay. I now left nothing behind that might have robbed me of my peace at a later date. All was well and taken care of.

As I settled in the airplane taking me to Europe for more than a year I was in awe at God's provision. How wonderfully He can order one's life. And I eagerly looked forward to seeing my children and my grandson again.

٭

I don't know if you are ever able to sleep in an airplane, especially, when you are looking forward to where you are going.

I tried. I listened to the radio; I dozed through the movie; I dutifully ate and drank as the stewardess brought the food and drink; I read and I knitted. If you sit on the right-hand side of the airplane going to Europe, you will, after a very short night, notice the sky getting lighter and lighter, until all of a sudden the glory of the risen sun bursts unto the horizon.... To the rising of the Sun, the name of the Lord shall be praised.... It was worth staying awake to see the beauty of the new day. Now it was only a short while before arriving in Frankfurt.

Was my family looking forward to see me as eagerly as I was to see them? Would Joey remember his Oma? As I came through customs, I knew that they were out there somewhere to meet me, and it was hard to wait. Finally the moment came when I saw them. It was a truly wonderful moment. I remember hearing this little voice saying, "Oma," and then there were big hugs and kisses. How good it is to love and be loved! Later in the evening Kathy confided that Joey, with one look, took in the entire situation and decided that he had a "cool" Oma. We were glad to see each other. I loved being with them and my beloved grandson Joey. For over a year he was my "roomie" in Frankfurt. Isn't it wonderful to be a grandma?

It was not very difficult for me to adjust to the language and the life in Germany, except for one thing. The noise in what was jokingly referred to as the "American ghetto": government housing. Especially during the warm months, when everyone's windows were open. Soon I was Oma to all the children in our row of apartment houses. It seemed they all missed their Oma, and the young women missed their mothers. I recall many sessions of lunch for a bunch of little kids where the favorite thing on the menu was Oma's pink and green and purple pancakes. They were truly awesome!

As the weeks went on, Kathy got bigger and bigger. After much walking back and forth to hasten the arrival. our baby was born on June 26, 1988. A girl, beautifully healthy: Christine, which means the anointed one.

Now, it was cuddling and diapers, and rocking and diapers; I had almost forgotten how that was! This time of nurturing Joey and loving both him and little Teenie was one of the most blessed times of my life and I daresay that many grandmothers would love to be able to do this, even though it is tough at times to put three generations under one roof for as long a time as I spent with the family. We were happy.

I met some very nice people. I found a very good church home. I was unsure of what the future held for me, except that I was busy and needed by my two grandchildren, which was pure joy for me. Never, however, did I forget the nudging that had come from God. Later there was a definite call. Now I was being reintroduced to the German culture, a prerequisite for what the Lord had in mind for me.

In November, I was totally amazed to be called by the president of a mission organization to meet with him as he came through Frankfurt on his way to Russia. I agreed to talk with him.

I borrowed the children's car and eagerly drove to the Frankfurt Airport Hotel Steigenberger to the meeting. I remember sitting in the lobby of the hotel waiting for the man's arrival. It was a very informal meeting where some of my questions were answered. I went back to our little flat not really knowing what it all meant.

I had earlier promised God, that I would not push for "ministry," ever. That, if He wanted me, I would go, but it would have to be very clear; I had seen too many people shipwreck spiritually because they were not sure of the Lord's will in their life and because not wanting to miss God, had pushed and were crushed. I was willing to wait on Him. This too was real training.

We celebrated Thanksgiving with the usual hustle and bustle. Then we prepared for a most wonderful Christmas in Austria, where I had very good friends. There we spent a most unforgettable Christmas vacation.

Kosovo, Christmas 1998
What terrible things were happening here every day. Oh Lord, how long will we be safe? It is cold, we have so little food, and Christmas is coming. Dear Lord, who protected the baby Jesus, protect us as well!

CHAPTER 25

Mission: Eastern Europe

FOR ME, THEY WERE REAL-LIVE MEMORIES of a Christmas many years ago at the end of a terrible war: 1945. This was another Christmas, 1988 in a small mountain village in Austria.

Oh, how the snow glittered in the sun and flew like a cloud of misty diamonds, when you went downhill on your skis. Every morning was like a new gift, sparkling clear in the warm sun. There was the celebration of the Christ child's coming on Christmas Eve, with oompah bands and a midnight mass. The Hausherr (head of the house) always read the Christmas story out of the Bible.

In the small baroque church the people were crowding in, and the smell of beeswax candles, the warmth of them, filled the room as the choir began the old and familiar "Silent Night." Sonnwend fires (solstice fires) were rolled down from the surrounding mountains. *Gloria in excelsis Deo!* The choir sang their praise of the maker of heaven and earth. Peace on Earth, Goodwill toward Man!

We ate typical Austrian Christmas food: a fish on Christmas Eve and a fatted goose on Christmas Day. There was a Christmas tree with real candles and sparklers. We went sledding; we watched the hang-gliders on skis land on the snowy meadows. We experienced all the things that I had remembered from my youth. It was good that my family saw, heard, and experienced a truly Austrian Christmas. It was a Christmas that none of my family will ever forget.

Spring came early this year. There never was much snow in Frankfurt. The many gardens in the city began to bloom and sprout. It was fun to go for daily walks with the two children without having to bundle the little one up. During the winter months we went for long walks even though it got quite cold.

There were the twice-a-week visits to the Christian bookstore for tapes and to buy a book for Joey's library. The almost-daily walk to the bakery and the little Automat in front of it, where those yummy gumballs were to be had!

Every so often I would take Joey on a subway ride to downtown Frankfurt, to the museum with the huge dinosaur or to the zoo. We went to German versions of classical children's shows where Mowgli was still Mowgli. It needed no interpretation because they were well known by Joey and easy to follow in the theater in the round. What fun!

There was the poring over the lighted globe to find the marvelous places we had read about in the Bible, places we had visited. We talked, and the eager questions of a young mind were answered.

We all enjoyed the museums of Germany, the music in the churches and concert halls, the parks and woods with all the walking paths. We went to the woods and picked chestnuts for our turkey dressing. We spent some of the weekends visiting Germany's beautiful art treasures in castles and churches. The cathedral where Martin Luther served, the Lorelei Rock on the Rhine River, the cathedral and the Roman baths in Trier, the cathedral of Cologne and many more. There was the Christkindl Market at Nürnberg, Würzburg, and the wonderful museum in Munich. There was Dachau, the concentration camp.

In February I went to Belgium, where I visited old friends, and right after my return I received another call from the Texas mission organization. Would I pick the president of the organization up at the airport? And so I did.

A meeting had been called for all the staff members working overseas. It was good to meet all of them, to have dinner with them, and to hear about the work being done. Later that spring I was called again, this time from Dallas, asking me to come to Denton, which is the home office, and receive computer training as well as office indoctrination. They needed a bilingual person who was sensitive to both the German and American culture, a person to organize the new office in southern Germany.

Was this what I had been trained for?

Vienna, Austria, 1999

I'm going to do it. I don't care who says what. I am going through with it. I know it is crazy to some people. To me it is real. This is my last thought about it. I am burning the bridges behind me. I have given up my home; my things; said goodbye to my family and friends…this is going to be a very long trip. Who knows when and how I will return. But it will be worth it. I will be fulfilling my dream. So long…

CHAPTER 26

A New Beginning

SO I PREPARED. As I did before, I met God half way. I decided what to leave in Frankfurt with friends, so I could pick it up when I returned, and what to take with me to the United States. In my own heart, I knew I would be back sometime in the late fall.

I was eager to find out what had happened with my home situation during the year I had been gone. Knowing that I would have to get training and be available for speaking engagements for the purpose of deputation, I purchased a ticket for June 29 to New Orleans. My children were scheduled to return to the United States in the middle of July. In particular, they thought that they would be going to Montgomery, Alabama. But, like everything in my life, it would prove to be different.

Flexibility...Preparedness.

The family took me to the airport. Frankfurt Airport was undergoing a major building program, and of course it immediately presented a parking problem, something one learns to live with in Europe. The plane that I was to be on was three hours late. It came from Hong Kong and I sat and waited. I noticed something very disturbing. As impatient as Europeans are on the roads, which, in most cases, have no speed limits, when it comes to waiting for planes and trains, there was no problem. It was the Americans who first whined and complained and then began to be demanding and outraged....We must be in control, mustn't we?

Flexibility...Preparedness.

Finally we moved closer to the given departure time, and, because of a bomb scare the week before, security was tight. One more check of everyone's hand luggage and purses. There it was again: "the very nerve." Well, I almost expected to hear someone say, "My congressman will hear about that," while the rest of the passengers just submitted to a routine that was intended to protect all of us. And again it flashed through my mind how totally out of control I was and how much God was in control. If we could just get this into our head, the easy way...

At last we were on the plane. Being three hours late, we wondered, would we make the plane connection in New York? How would we let our loved ones know who came to pick us up at the destination of our travel. What a silly thought! They would find out if we were not on the plane.

Besides, there was nothing any of us could do about it. Oh well, whatever, Lord...aha, I am learning.... Flexibility.

After a few hours' flight, New York! A sea of lights with the outline of Manhattan clearly came in view. We circled the city to land at Kennedy Airport. It became apparent that most of us, who had a few hours of layover, would make our connections, and so all of the worrying made little difference. I remember once reading in Corrie Ten Boom's book that one didn't need one's ticket till one got on the train. Oh, Lord how true: "Be anxious for nothing." Why is it so hard in the little things to remember this, when in the big things of our life we are quite willing to trust the Lord?

In New Orleans my friends, my Alabama family, waited. Soon we went toward "home."

Immediately, I was caught up in a swirl of seeing people; greeting old friends, having dinner with them, sharing what God had put on my heart. Showing off pictures of grandchildren and children and places and cities and friends. I also immediately began to share the Mission's work with friends and interested groups, for the purpose of raising support and involvement.

This was a very hard thing for me to do. Up until now, I had mostly been a giver and not much of a taker. God knew there was this pride thing involved and a total submitting to the Lord's control, for my provision, was required. I needed this training to be made a member of a team. The Body at work. And as much as I had to battle this, to me, very unpleasant task, I did it in obedience to my superiors. It was expected of me. I knew the Lord had a lesson for me to learn. It became a blessing. I never turned down any invitation to speak, be it two or two hundred people listening. By now I knew that the money for me would be there, because it was no longer I who was the arranger. I know that it was equally pleasing to the people who committed themselves to giving by underwriting either my work or the Mission itself.

In August, I was to be taken to Denton, Texas, by friends. But before we could leave, there was a medical emergency. A serious heart surgery that had to be done. Someone else in the Body jumped in the breach and took me. He drove almost two days in order to serve. My friend's heart was repaired by this medical emergency. How we thanked the Lord!

I spent two weeks in Texas. With friends. Earlier they had a great impact on my life. It was through their teaching that I had reached an understanding of the Word that prepared me for what was to be in my life. May the Lord bless them.

While I was there I took a sixteen-hour crash course in computer science. (Read, it was crammed into my head. I hoped to be able to sort it out when the time came.) I was taught the things needed to be able to do the work in Germany. Help, Lord, I thought. This was an entirely new experience for me. I got to know my coworkers, their hearts. I saw the real desire to serve God where He had put us. The unity of people of different denominations for the sake of the work of the Lord. The intensity of prayers on behalf of the ones serving in Europe and the United States. I was given some forms to sign: releases of the Mission's responsibility for my safety; a contract with the Mission, which bound me to them for at least two years, an agreement that I would not, through the Mission's contacts, start my own missionary program; an application for a medical insurance program that was needed in order to receive permission to work in Europe; and an application for a residence visa to enter West Germany.

I further read all the other instructions in two books, one concerning my deputation for support with the biblical root for it and the other one concerning the management of one's life while in Europe. The non-involvement in political affairs; the non-involvement in denominational controversy, the required daily reading and study of the Word of God, the required blending into the community one lived in and the church community as well. The discipline one was to expect if the requirements were not adhered to...."Bring honor to your father" went through my mind. Only now it was my heavenly Father. I was put on insurance and salary as of September. I was ready for service. I never knew so much was involved in going on the mission rield.

After two weeks two lady friends came to Denton to pick me up. We had a wonderful time traveling together back to Alabama.

Now the nitty-gritty work started. Dental exam; blood work; x-rays; a strict physical exam geared to working in stress-related areas.

Then came the international driver's license and the certification that I was debt free; the Consulate General of West Germany required more paperwork, including passport pictures. I had a dozen made.

Meanwhile, back at the ranch, my children were finally coming home to the States. Only six weeks later than they thought and, as befits Uncle Sam, to Fort Hood in Killeen, Texas, instead of Montgomery, Alabama. They too had to learn a few things about control. I had prayed for them. You want to watch what you pray for when you pray for your children!

They had rented a little car for the trip from New York to Texas, and they were going to pick me up on the way. We needed to find a place to live and get settled; that is, I would do the babysitting while they looked. Without their knowledge, the car they had rented had been promised to someone who insisted on driving it. So the agency, full of excuses, promised to come pick up the car and bring them a different one before they left. They did: A Lincoln Continental—big enough to live in, after the European compacts we had been used to.

We traveled in style; it was wonderful with five of us in the car. In Houston we picked up the car that had been shipped from Germany. We bought a roof luggage rack and installed it. On a steaming-hot day we continued our trip in a small car without cooling. Ach well, as they would say in Scotland or Germany or wherever.

We were really fortunate, we thought, because we found a house almost immediately and within a week were settled in with the furniture shipment that had arrived from Germany. I knew that their home from now on would always be my home, and so I invested in the purchase of the property. I was happy for them. My grandchildren found friends and we found a kindergarten for Joey. The children made the acquaintance of a neighborhood dog. They named the dog Mike even though it turned out to be a Michelle. They were content and this made me feel good.

I returned to Mobile. From there I went on speaking engagements in different towns and different churches. It was going on for four months now and there was still no word on the situation of my home. I almost thought I would have to leave without getting this hurdle taken care of. But God....He never gets in a hurry as I would. One day I received a message. It was from the occupants of my home. I knew, that I knew, that I knew... And so it was. Their home had sold, and they were ready to fulfill their commitment to me. They had put a lot of work and money into the house and were eager to complete the paperwork because the home was still in my name. I am glad that there is still trust between people, and I thank the Lord that He had let me experience it in this way.

All the paperwork was drawn up. We adjusted the price according to our agreement, and now we had to wait, again. I had a last commitment to appear on a small TV station in Mobile before leaving.

I was numb from all the constant changing of locations, from making adjustments. Every day brought new challenges. Good training!

And then came the day when I had to leave. I would be gone for at least two years. I had become an intricate part of my Alabama family. It was hard to say goodbye to them all. Would I ever see them again? God bless them, please, while I am gone.

My next destination was Austin, Texas, from where my son Paul picked me up. And again the plane was late. Poor Joey began to cry: they had lost his Oma! But I did get there, just a little late. I was to spend the next weeks with Paul, Kathy, and the two grandchildren and enjoy their companionship.

My departure date was set for December 7, and it was fast approaching. Before I left we celebrated our own Christmas. We had our traditional open house with newly made and old friends who came to celebrate with us. We took time to visit with each other, to see the countryside, and to find out where the ducks and chickens came from one morning, as we looked out the window. There was a farm close by. We flew kites on the wide-open field opposite the house and we watched the dog "Mike" chasing some critters. It was good family time.

My other son and his wife, who live in Florida, called to say goodbye and to tell me they were glad I was going. I was happy to have their approval. Now both of my children supported the work I was about to do, and I knew I had to hold loosely those I loved. It is not an easy thing.

And as the day of my departure approached, we were still waiting for all the paperwork for my home. Would it come in time? Paul and I decided what to do with the money if I was gone by the time it came. We had a power of attorney made that gave him the authority to act on my behalf. This money was to be invested for my retirement. Long ago it had become clear to me that I was not to use this money to maintain my living while I was out of the country. In the next week the Federal Express carrier literally went back and forth between his office and our home, and as I got ready to leave the morning of the seventh of December, all we were waiting for was the check for the money of the sale. It came within one hour of my departure. Talk about getting the ticket when you need it!

It was very hard to leave and give a hug and a kiss to Kathy, Christine, and Joey and say goodbye to Paul. I had gotten used to family life in the United States. From now on I yearned for the States while in Europe, and I yearned for Europe when in the States. My home is nowhere, and everywhere. I will miss them. I will miss all of you. May the Lord bless and keep you, till I see you again.

I got on the commuter plane in Killeen, Texas, where my children had brought me, to make the plane connection to Dallas. I knew that a part of my life had ended and would never be the same again. That there was a new one, out there somewhere in the making, and I wanted it to be a good one, full of fruit, bringing pleasure to Him. With these thoughts, I never noticed how small that little plane was that took me out into the unknown, where only God had control.

In my beginning there was God.

In Dallas, I began to move toward the gate where my plane to Europe would take off. Talk about a city within a city! It took a long time to get to the departure gate for my final flight. And when I got there, my wonderful pastor friends stood there, waiting for me, eagerly wanting to hear my plans for the near future. We talked and visited, I was properly prayed over, and finally it was time for them to leave, and I was left to my thoughts. How strangely my life had turned this way and that, only to arrive at a place where He would have His way in it. I knew that this was the plan that we all talk about in many a Christian conversation and prayer, the plan for me, even though I did not really understand it all.

After my arrival in Frankfurt, I quickly picked up a car and the boxes I had left behind and began my drive to Bergen in Bavaria. It was a beautiful sunny winter morning with glistening ice crystals on the ground and in the trees.

Many times in the future I would arrive just like that morning at the airport and begin my trip "home" to Bergen. It is thrilling to see the beauty of the Alps rising before you. Row after row of beautiful snow-covered peaks. The icy-blue glaciers sparkling in the winter sun.

As I arrived in Bergen and drove through it, I noticed the neat, clean buildings. Homes that were cared for, and I wondered where it was that I would be living.

I checked in with my contact there, and, after having a cup of coffee, I was taken to a local inn, where a room had been reserved for me until such a time that I could find some other accommodation.

Bergen is a most pleasant place, quiet. Just before the Christmas holidays, it is fully decorated. The food that I tasted that evening was delicious and more than enough. It did not take much for me to fall asleep. Upon awakening, the next morning, I realized the full beauty of my surroundings. From my balcony I could see the majesty of the mountains all around me. I gave thanks to my Lord.

The very first day I found an apartment, which, to say the least, is not an easy undertaking here in Germany. There is never enough rental property for people, it seems. But God knew.

He led me into a store to inquire, and lo and behold! the owner herself had a small apartment, usually rented to vacationers. She was willing to rent it to me till the first of May. We agreed on a price that was feasible for me, and so it was that on the second day here I moved in and began to be settled. It was a very satisfying arrangement for both of us. They had their first vacationer coming on the first of May, and the Mission building under construction was to be ready on the first of May. Part of my job was to oversee, with the help of a very knowledgeable German gentleman, the progress of the construction. When it was finished it was a lovely Bavarian building that housed the office and several apartments for the American missionaries.

I was getting accustomed to files and works and things having to do with the ministry here before my coworker left for the United States for a three-month furlough. On the tenth of December I took him to the Airport in Munich. Coming home, I was driving a Land Rover with four-wheel drive and a five-speed stick shift, in a part of the city I was not familiar with, on a snowy road in pure glorious sunshine.

Be flexible, Marlene...

The very next day my other two coworkers got ready to go to Romania and fulfill their commitment there before going on their furlough to the USA. They brought the computer into the little kitchen. I now had an office-kitchen-dining-sitting room; how exciting! There was only one problem: a file one morning had drippings of jelly on it. I had a sleeping room that was a copy machine–storage room as well. My foyer contained boxes and a heater and coats. But there was always the bathroom. Everyone knows that one has to store things somewhere. I had been trained!

For the first time in thirty-six years I had Christmas with my brother who lived about one-and-a-half hours drive from Bergen. Coming back I pondered, was this part of the reason I was over here, Lord?

But I had no time to pursue this thought any more, because my coworkers were still not home from the hell that was Temeshvar, Romania. Oh, dear Lord, so close to their furlough, give them favor with man, keep them safe. And He did. They were led away from the place of destruction in some very peculiar way. They arrived back here safely. Four days later they left to go on furlough. Yet another goodbye, a change of cars from the Land Rover to a Volkswagen Santana, five on the floor.

Be flexible, Marlene...

And there I was. Totally by myself. No telephone, because it is very hard to get one. I had flashbacks to the days of World War II when there were no phones and I could not get in touch with my family. I knew I was not alone. It kept me sane.

I had made contact with a German Evangelische Freie Kirche (Evangelical Free Church). I attended their church service and their Bible study. I visited a young woman with four children who had the flu very badly; I enjoyed talking with my landlord and landlady, with the grocer, the butcher, the postman. I was being absorbed into the community. No longer was I my own.

The building that the Mission was constructing came along very nicely, and by the first of May I moved into my apartment and set up the office. I was busy organizing and becoming familiar with the work in the East: to assist the still suffering church in the Eastern European countries. There is a lot of work to be done, while there is time, while the borders are open. It might not be long. Who knows?

I no longer have an encumbrance. I am free to move according to the master plan. Many times in strange places, meeting strange people, I feel the urgency of that last call of the trumpet. I will always be awed at the miracles, the grace of our Lord, the perfect timing for all things concerning his servants.

The many years of preparation are coming to fruition. My longing is stilled, my search is over. I know my place and I know who had planned it all for me. I have learned that I don't have to know all there is to know. He is the Potter and I am the clay. And that is enough.

Epilogue

I HAVE CELEBRATED MY SEVENTIETH BIRTHDAY. As I look back on my life, I am amazed by all I have witnessed during the years, and how I have noticed a whole society change.

For today's people my life might have been a very hard one but I know that there were people much worse off than I ever was. It is all of the little and big events I saw and lived through that have shaped the person I am today. Some of the hardest things I went through were the strongest lessons for my daily walk today. Every hardship built perseverance into me. Every sadness made me stronger. Every joy made me appreciate life more. No one ever knows joy unless he has also experienced great tribulation in his life.

Today, I am glad to be alive and able to share some of the treasures life has deposited into me. I have learned to embrace unpleasantness and deal with it. I have learned to be flexible and to throw out my expectations of others. I have put away fear. I rely on the Lord, who has been my sole provider. I have learned that He never fails me.

This is the story of my life. If at times it seemed far removed from what you are experiencing, let me assure you, it is relevant to everyone who reads it. You see, all through my life I have had a need for Christ. You, dear reader, are no different. You need Him as much as I do. I want to pass on the love that has been poured out unto me by my Maker. Life is good. There is hope. We can make it.

In the past few years, since my retirement, I have traveled often to Bulgaria and other countries by request of various missionary groups. To say that my old age is dull would be an outright lie! Every time I spend two or three months in Eastern Europe I know I am where God wants me to be. There are many stories to tell. Some funny, some sad. Some are heartwarming; others are miracles of God. But never are they dull.

I wish to write about them and let you see the hand of God at work in my next book entitled *Crossing the Threshold*.

We enjoy security, and it almost seems that we think it is our inherited right. But the truth is that the very security and peace we enjoy is extremely fragile. It must be treasured and nurtured. We are fortunate in this country that we are free to write about the things we have experienced, even when our views are not popular. I want to take advantage of that privilege.

There was a time when I could not have done that. The ominous claw that held so many of us captive has been shattered, and no longer do we have to fear it.

But beware, because the vulture is still very much alive seeking its next victim.